Semiotics and Popular

Series Editor
Marcel Danesi
University of Toronto
Toronto, ON, Canada

Semiotics and Popular Culture aims to show the contemporary relevance of cultural theory and present difficult concepts in a clear, jargon-free style. Written by leading figures in the three interconnected fields of media, popular culture, and semiotic studies, this series is an exercise in unraveling the socio-psychological reasons why certain cultural trends become popular. It intends to engage theory and technology and expose its subject matter in a clear, open, and meaningful way.

More information about this series at
http://www.palgrave.com/gp/series/14487

Marcel Danesi

The Semiotics of Love

palgrave
macmillan

Marcel Danesi
Department of Anthropology
University of Toronto
Toronto, ON, Canada

Semiotics and Popular Culture
ISBN 978-3-030-18110-9   ISBN 978-3-030-18111-6   (eBook)
https://doi.org/10.1007/978-3-030-18111-6

This Palgrave Macmillan imprint is published by the registered company Springer Nature Switzerland AG
The registered company address is: Gewerbestrasse 11, 6330 Cham, Switzerland

Preface

Who so loves believes the impossible.
—Elizabeth Barrett Browning (1806–1861)

Since antiquity, humans everywhere have been fascinated with the origin and nature of love. Throughout the world and across time, we have developed special language, rituals, symbols, art forms, songs, and courtship practices to enact, celebrate, and acknowledge its emotional power over us and its ability to shape the destiny of individuals. In a phrase, love has been a universal preoccupation since the dawn of history, and continues to be so even in an age where science, technology, and artificial intelligence are believed to have the capacity to solve all human problems and unravel all mysteries, including the puzzle of love. But love remains a conundrum, seemingly just beyond the grasp of our understanding. Trying to unravel what it means to us with the tools of the science of semiotics—the science of meaning—is the objective of this book.

Although love is experienced more or less in the same way the world over, it has produced diverse interpretations that vary in context, while retaining a basic cognitive essence for everyone. It is deciphering those interpretations that mostly concerns a "semiotics of love," that is, an approach that seeks to understand love through the signs, symbols, and other meaning-bearing structures that people have used to express it throughout time. How we have written about love, how we have depicted it in music and visual images, how we have symbolized it, how we have ritualized it, and how we have philosophized about it, provide the "semiotic data" for grasping its overall meaning and function in human life. The specific approach used here is based on the notion that we convert our feelings into sign structures (words, symbols, etc.)

and sign-based constructions (texts, rituals, etc.), which then allow us to reflect upon them consciously, rather than just intuitively. This book will not utilize the complex theoretical apparatus of semiotics, but rather its broader perspective of seeking to understand what love means through a consideration of the forms used to represent it (language, narratives, poetry, symbolism, rituals, etc.). It is written for a general readership, but with an eye towards making the study of love an area of interest among semioticians as well, given that there is, as of yet, no extensive semiotic treatment of this topic. The brilliant 1977 work by the late French semiotician Roland Barthes, *A Lover's Discourse: Fragments*, is not, strictly speaking, a semiotic study. It consists of a list of "fragments" that Barthes selected from literature and philosophy in order to provide *pensées* on love from various viewpoints.

Love is, of course, intertwined physically and emotionally with sex. The two form a semiotic opposition, which is an intrinsic property of all human conceptual systems—that is, we determine the meaning of something not in isolation, but in a relation to something else. An opposition does not mean that love and sex are opposites, but rather that we understand one in terms of the other (as will be discussed). This is why sexual images tend to be carnal and erotic; romantic ones idyllic and idealistic; why sex can be performed in erotic spectacles, while love can be realized with acts such as romantic kissing; and so on. Moreover, as in all semiotic oppositions, the love-sex one itself interacts with other related oppositions—above all else, it is connected to the sacred and profane opposition; that is, love is sensed to be a manifestation of the spiritual (sacred) within us, and sex of the carnal (profane). Our representations bear out this fundamental conceptualization and guide our understanding of what the two emotional forces mean in our lives.

Sex is a survival instinct, but we have "semiotized" it, rendering it meaningful in specific ways, thus displacing it from the domain of the instincts and raising it up to conscious reflection through erotic stories, sculptures, spectacles, and the like. Love, too, has a biological basis—it is a product of sensory and affective structures. But, again, we have extracted it from the body and raised it up to the level of consciousness through specific kinds of representations that stand in opposition to the sexual ones (love poetry, love symbols, etc.). All this shows, ultimately, is that we live not only in the biosphere, but also in what the Tartu School semiotician Yuri Lotman called the *semiosphere*, a universe of signs and sign structures that we have constructed to allow us to think about the world, rather than just react instinctively to it.

Men and women alike desire sex equally, but we tend to believe that the genders "naturally" experience it differently. So, certain misconceptions have developed over time about what "men and women want." In some societies, men have traditionally been expected to be the "sex-seekers," to initiate court-ship, and to show an aggressive interest in women; but in others, such as some indigenous societies of North America, these very same roles and passions are expected of the women. In modern-day urban societies, gender roles are reversing or equalizing, as people are freer than ever before to determine their own sexual and romantic agendas, separate from their gender identities and sexual orientations. There is one constant, however, that cuts across all cultures and sexual orientations. Love (when and if it comes) is genderless; it descends upon people, no matter their sexuality. Already in the early 1930s, American anthropologist Margaret Mead had collected data on romantic behavior in island cultures, discovering that although courtship practices were gendered, the people all seemed to share a basic desire—the need for love.

The universality of love may be the reason why so many stories and myths about it exist. In Guanajuato, Mexico, there is place called El Callejón del Beso, The Alley of the Kiss, which, according to legend, was once the final scene of a tragic love affair, recalling other archetypal stories, such as the Romeo and Juliet one. It is said that two lovers met there to elope, but when the woman's father discovered their plot, he stabbed his daughter in the heart. As she lay dying, her lover kissed her for the last time. From this last desperate gesture of romantic love, the alley received its name. It is reported that anyone who kisses in the alley is guaranteed seven years of happiness and fortune. Stories of star-crossed lovers like this one abound. They show that we perceive love as both a bonding and a deconstructive force, not just a physical act, like sex. It is something that impels us to go against traditions and even common sense, risking our own lives in order to consummate it. Love may thus be a significant semiotic key to understanding human nature. That will be the main theme that I intend to pursue throughout this book.

I dedicate this book to my lifelong partner of over half a century, Lucia. She was my first and is the love of my life. I cannot imagine life without her.

Toronto, ON, Canada

Marcel Danesi

Contents

List of Figures

1

Conceptualizing Love

Love is everything it's cracked up to be.
—Erica Jong (b. 1942)

Prologue

The unmistakable feeling that we call *love* in English seems to descend on us out of nowhere when we least expect it, even though we may not want it, since it alters how we will subsequently live our lives. It is an irresistible inner force. Unlike the set of biological urges that we call *sex*, and which we can indulge and gratify through carnal activities, love keeps us on an emotional leash that defies common sense. Of course, love and sex often go together, with one influencing the other, physiologically and emotionally. Since the beginning of time people have nonetheless constantly conceptualized love as being separate from sex, and thus, a departure from our animal instincts—that is, as something unique that transcends our biology. In many species, sexual desire is stimulated by signals emitted during estrus (a recurring period of sexual receptivity and fertility). People experience desire outside of any fixed biological period, which induces them to pursue sexual activities at any time. In acknowledgment of the universal differentiation felt to exist between love and sex, Italian Renaissance philosopher Marsilio Ficino coined the term "Platonic love," alluding to love as a divine or spiritual force that is different from sex and that can exist separately from it.[1]

© The Author(s) 2019
M. Danesi, *The Semiotics of Love,* Semiotics and Popular Culture,
https://doi.org/10.1007/978-3-030-18111-6_1

Animals may also experience a form of love, but we can never be sure what "love" in different species means because we tend to interpret emotional responses in animals in human terms. Charles Darwin wrote about chimpanzees displaying courtship behaviors that seemed very similar to human romantic ones.[2] However, it is a stretch to assume that the two are identical, although they certainly are comparable. In her classic book, *In the Shadow of Man*, the renowned primatologist Jane Goodall writes about two apes as follows: "I saw one female, newly arrived in a group, hurry up to a big male and hold her hand toward him. Almost regally he reached out, clasped her hand in his, drew it toward him, and kissed it with his lips."[3] Again, the description makes sense in human terms, unconsciously assuming an equivalency between humans and apes. Different species share certain life schemas with humans, and these may involve overlapping emotional qualities. But equating them is risky. As the biologist Jakob von Uexküll argued in his pivotal work on the animal mind, we can never really know what animals truly think and feel; we can only compare their behaviors to ours and make projections and analogies.[4] Animals display astounding intelligence, emotions, creativity, and other traits that sometimes appear to overlap with human ones. And they may indeed possess a form of love that is analogous to human love. But all we can do is compare it to ours, interpreting it on our own terms, not on their behalf.

Many of the ancient mythic stories dealt expressively with the emotional tug between love and sex in ways that implied that this opposition was directive of human destiny. For instance, Aphrodite, the Greek goddess of love and beauty (Venus in Roman mythology), represented the interplay between spiritual love and sexual seduction through the various stories told about her. In Homer, Aphrodite was married to Hephaestus, the blacksmith of the gods. But many other stories give her other lovers, including Ares, the god of war, and the Trojan prince Anchises. In later myths, she was also portrayed as the mother of the love god Eros. Her counterpart was Diana, the moon goddess representing various aspects of women's lives, including childbirth. Diana symbolized chastity and modesty. When Actaeon saw her bathing—a voyeuristic sexual act—she took revenge on him by changing him into a stag. He was immediately attacked and killed by hounds, an act of divine retribution for violating the purity of love. Aphrodite and Diana are mythic figures standing for the intrinsic opposition, yet intricate relation, between sex and love, sensuality and tenderness, the sacred and the profane.

The early myths begged an abiding question that still plagues human consciousness: What is love? Even finding a surface definition is virtually impossible. All we can do, plausibly, is document and examine the multitude of expressive artifacts (words, symbols, stories, myths, poetry, etc.) it has enfolded throughout time. In its romantic sense—which is the one that is of interest in this book—it stands for a feeling of intense, passionate desire toward someone. It is perceived commonly as irrational, impelling individuals "in love" to act in ways that are unconventional and even perilous. The ancient Greek philosophers actually identified six forms of love—*eros* (sexual love), *philia* (love of friends), *ludus* (playful love), *agape* (spiritual love), *pragma* (longstanding love), and *philautia* (love of the self). It was the opposition and interconnection between *eros* and *agape* that found its way into the plots of many of the early stories. *Pragma* also played a role in them, but not as prominently. As the late psychoanalyst Erich Fromm cogently argued, we have always assigned too much importance to "falling in love," rather than *pragma*, or "standing in love," thus failing to make an effort to give love rather than just receive it.[5] Of course, it could well be that *pragma* emanates from *agape*, at least when it "works out," to use a common metaphorical depiction of this truly enigmatic emotion.

Ancient Views

One of the most widely-known myths based on the love-sex opposition is the story of Cupid in Roman mythology, identified with the Greek god Eros. Cupid was one of Venus' sons, and in one version his story is all about the antagonistic emotional tug between love and sex, cruelty and joy. Cupid's cruelty is manifest in his treatment of his wife, the beautiful princess Psyche. He forbade her ever to try seeing what he looked like, refusing to be with her except at night in the dark. One night, as Cupid slept, Psyche lit a lamp so she could take a look at him. He awoke and fled in anger, abandoning his beloved, becoming heartbroken and taking out his anger on others, by either uniting or dividing them romantically with his arrows, allowing fate to determine which of the two would be realized. The myth of Cupid is essentially an ancient imaginative treatise on the ambiguities, incongruities, and contrastive vicissitudes that we associate with love and sex. As D. H. Lawrence once put it, our tales of love are antidotes to our disappointments and delusions: "And what's romance? Usually, a nice little tale where you have everything *As You Like It*, where rain never wets your jacket and gnats never bite your nose and it's always daisy-time."[6]

Along with the story-tellers, the ancient philosophers became intrigued with the meaning of love and especially how it may have originated in our species. In the fifth century BCE, Empedocles saw love as a physical force that causes the elements in the universe to come together as compounds, counteracting a force that he called "strife," which causes the compounds to break up. He believed that the universe undergoes a continuous cycle from complete unification under the domination of love to complete separation under strife, and that this cycle occurs in humans as well after they experience love and its delusions.[7] Some philosophers saw love, instead, as a form of madness—a perception that extends right through to modern times, as can be seen in our popular discourse about love ("madly in love," "crazy in love," "to lose one's mind," etc.). In Plato's *Symposium*, written between 385 and 370 BCE,[8] love is portrayed as an obsession by the guests at Plato's imaginary banquet, since it arouses irrational passions that could lead to illogical self-immolating behaviors. At the banquet, the playwright Aristophanes ascribes love to a revenge of the gods. Originally, he claims, humanity had a tripartite nature—some people were male, some were female, and others half male and half female. This made humanity strong and resistant to the will of the gods. As a result, the latter intervened to set the conditions that defined our fallible sexual nature—males searching for males, females searching for females, and males and females searching for each other.

The theme of love-as-an-obsession was a dominant one in Greek literary history as well. One of the most famous stories was the one of Helen of Troy. During an absence of her husband, Menelaus, the king of Sparta, Helen fled to Troy with Paris, son of the Trojan king Priam, in betrayal of her husband. After Paris was slain, she married his brother Deiphobus, whom she also betrayed when Troy was subsequently captured. Such behavior was irrational, yet it occurred because of the power of love to possess people's hearts and alter their destinies. In the *Iliad*, the farewell scene between Hector and Andromache is similarly a tragic paean to love's emotional control over people, as are the romantic episodes describing the love of Kalypsó for Odysseus in the *Odyssey*. Sappho's poetry likewise deals with the overwhelming sway of love to change human fate indelibly. The dramas of the three great Greek playwrights, Aeschylus, Sophocles, and Euripides invariably dealt with the fateful actions of legendary gods and goddesses, and of heroes and heroines on stage, many of whom were tragically entangled in love trysts, love triangles, and romantic betrayals.

The Bible is also replete with stories of both the spiritual nature of true love and of sexual mischief. In the narratives of Isaac and Rebekah, Boaz and Ruth, and Zechariah and Elizabeth, love is portrayed as part of God's plan, joining those couples predestined to be together, keeping them united happily and humbly as a family. The subtext is the value and importance of marriage and family as institutions created by God and which exist to give God praise and glory. Our expression "a love made in heaven" traces its source to this ancient subtext. But the Bible also describes the other side of love—obsession, madness, and betrayal spurred on by lust. In the *Second Book of Samuel* there is a story of a woman tempting a man by kissing him passionately on the lips; he cannot help but give in to his passions, losing his mind in the process. The story of Samson and Delilah, among others, dealt similarly with the destructive power of love. Samson was the strongest man on earth, but his downfall came when he fell in love with Delilah, a Philistine woman. She learned that the secret of his strength lay in his long hair, and so she had his head shaved while he slept. As a result, Samson was captured and made to work as a slave. At the festival of the god Dagon, when the temple was filled with people, the Philistines led Samson into the temple so that the crowd could hurl ridicule at him. But his hair had grown back, so he seized the pillars that supported the roof and pulled the building down, killing himself and thousands of his enemies. As Jennifer Wright Knust has cogently argued, biblical tales such as these acknowledge the seductive allure of carnal seduction, juxtaposing it against the unifying power of spiritual love.[9] Michael Coogan suggests, in fact, that the Bible is a kind of vicarious treatise on love and sexual relations and what they tell us about human nature and its fallibility.[10]

Ancient poetry emerged as a kind of "natural language of love"—a perception that has spawned traditions that persist to this day, such as writing poetry to our paramours or buying them poetic sentiments written on cards on occasions such as Valentine's Day. The passions and sufferings caused by love are proclaimed forcefully in the epic poem, *Argonautica*, written by Apollonius Rhodius in the third century BCE, which recounts the legend of the voyage of Jason and the Argonauts to retrieve the Golden Fleece from Colchis. The desperate and obsessive love of Medea for Jason is what transforms her physically and emotionally, leading to ruin and tragedy[11]:

> Her heart fell from out her bosom, and a dark mist came over her eyes, and a hot blush covered her cheeks. And she had no strength to lift her knees backwards or forwards, but her feet beneath were rooted to the ground; and meantime all her handmaidens had drawn aside. So they two stood face to face without a word, without a sound, like oaks or lofty pines, which stand quietly side by side on the mountains when the wind is still; then again, when stirred by the breath of the wind, they murmur ceaselessly; so they two were destined to tell out all their tale, stirred by the breath of Love.

Jason and Medea had two children and lived happily in Corinth for ten years. But Jason then fell in love with Creusa, the daughter of the king of Corinth, abandoning his wife for her. In revenge, Medea gave her rival a magic robe that burned Creusa to death when she put it on. Medea then killed the two sons she had by Jason, fleeing to Athens. No emotion other than love, not even the desire for fame and fortune, could have motivated someone to perpetrate such horrific deeds of revenge. Medea is the central character in tragedies by Euripides and the Roman author Seneca. Her story is also retold in *Medée* (1635) by Pierre Corneille of France, in *Medea* (1946) by the American poet Robinson Jeffers, and by many others.

The more gentle and seductive part of love is a counterpart theme in ancient poetry, as can be found, for example, in the works of the first-century Roman writer Catullus who describes love as a kind of magical compulsion. His best-known poem, *To Lesbia*, tells of his desire for an aristocratic Roman woman called Clodia whom he named Lesbia in his poetry. In Song 5, he writes[12]:

> Give me a thousand kisses
> a hundred more, another thousand, and another hundred,
> and, when we've counted up the many thousands,
> confuse them so as not to know them all,
> so that no enemy may cast an evil eye,
> by knowing that there were so many kisses.

Significantly, the kissing takes place after the setting of the sun, which is likely to be an allusion to death, and love itself is portrayed as a magical force that offers protection against the evil eye. Kissing is a unification of body and soul, sex and love—as Catullus observes, they are "confused" in a way that can only be understood poetically. Catullus's poetry was his attempt to come to grips with his love affair with the married Clodia from its hopeful beginning to its final disillusionment. In it, the force of love to overwhelm him comes through, as can be seen by his obsession over kisses (a hundred, another thousand, and so on).

The poetry of Lucretius also refers to love as an irresistible force that has its basis in carnal passion[13]:

> They grip, they squeeze, their humid tongues they dart,
> As each would force their way t'other's heart.

The poem appears in Lucretius' *De rerum natura* ("On the Nature of Things"), which is a philosophical treatment that he wrote to argue against superstition and the fear of death. Lucretius was inspired by the writings of the Greek philosopher Epicurus, and the work reflects the Epicurean ideals of a tranquil mind and freedom from irrational fear through unbridled pleasure-seeking. Aware of the power of love to lead men astray, yet another Roman poet, Ovid, advises male suitors in his *Ars amatoria* ("The Art of Love") to gain control of love as follows[14]:

> Kiss, if you can: resistance if she make,
> And will not give you kisses, let her take.
> Fie, fie, you naughty man, and of course;
> She struggles but to be subdued by force.

Ovid's warning is difficult to interpret from a modern perspective. Is he advising men to take advantage of women? The *Ars amatoria* is a love manual in verse. Two of its three books are addressed to men and one to women. All three are written in a humorous, satirical style. So, it is likely that Ovid is making fun of masculine lovemaking, not sanctioning it.

One of the most comprehensive ancient treatments of love as an irresistible psychic force comes from Vedic poetry, which may go as far back as 1500 BCE India, where we read of lovers "sniffing" and "smelling" each other, suggesting a carnal basis to the love emotion.[15] However, the poems also praise spiritual love among couples as the ideal for achieving happiness and even success in life. So, *eros* is seen as part of *pragma*, and perhaps the only true means for guaranteeing a happy marriage or relationship. The Vedic model of romantic love is believed to have been exported westward by Alexander the Great after conquering the Punjab in 326 BCE, remaining the idealistic model for successful marriage that has remained unbroken to this day.[16] In the *Kama Sutra*, a Sanskrit treatise on the art of love and sex, written around the third century CE, *agape* and *eros* are seen as complements of each other.[17] Love must be sexual, but also moderate and soft as the romantic relationship proceeds toward becoming permanent. Interestingly, the notion of love-as-madness does not appear in these wise Indian texts, as it does in other parts of the world. Clearly, love has many interpretations, even though these rest on a common ground of meaning whereby love is a mysterious spiritual force that defies any rational explanation.

The Chivalric Code

The ancient myths, love stories, dramas, and poems dealt with romantic trysts among gods and goddesses, heroes and heroines, or enlightened philosophers and poets.[18] They rarely dealt with love among common people, suggesting implicitly that love was something that descended upon "noble" beings, often immortal or immortalized, not ordinary folk. This view changed gradually after the advent of the chivalric code and the poetry of "courtly love" that it engendered during the medieval period.[19] The theme of unbridled love, free from the yoke of traditions, independent of social class, has permeated world-wide groupthink ever since. Love as an experience for one and all has, in effect, become a universal principle of human existence.

People of all social stripes in the Middle Ages not only started searching for everlasting love, but also had trysts in secret, outside of marriage. Love had become "free," prefiguring the open love movement of the hippie 1960s. The poetry and paintings of the era started to capture and convey this new con-sciousness of love, as the painting below shows, titled *Duke and Ladies in a Garden*, by Christine de Pizan, which she completed around 1410. It is a portrait of what love was thought to be ideally all about—gentlemen and ladies associating freely in a garden, openly expressing their love interests. The painter lived in the early 1400s; she was an Italian writer and artist, who wrote a radical book for the era, *The Book of the City of Ladies and The Treasure of the City of Ladies*, in which she defended women's right to be themselves, free from the moral strictures imposed on them by authority figures (Fig. 1.1):

The rules of the new love game were even codified, so that everyone could play by them equally, not just the "Dukes" and their "ladies". In *De amore*

Fig. 1.1 *Duke and Ladies in a Garden (Christine de Pizan, c. 1410)* (Wikimedia Commons)

("The Art of Courtly Love"), written in 1185 by a certain Andreas Capellanus, there is a passage describing what a successful marriage entailed—not a simple business transaction between families, but a romantic bond (*pragma*) that should exist forever and forged by the lovers themselves (*agape*), independently of social expectations. Interestingly, Capellanus concedes to human weakness, allowing for jealousy to be a motivator of the love code: "Marriage is no real excuse for not loving, because who is not jealous cannot love."[20] The Renaissance philosopher Giovanni Pico della Mirandola wrote, a few centuries later, in a similar vein about the importance of romantic partners displaying their feelings openly and remaining united spiritually in his *Commentary on a Love Song*, written in 1486: "pouring out their souls one into the other with kisses, they will not exchange their souls so much as perfectly unite together, so that each of them may be said to be two souls and both of them one soul only."[21]

Before the advent of the chivalric code, marriage was essentially a transaction between families or a form of barter. In the city of Florence, for instance, there is a striking gate called *Porta Romana*, making up part of the outer circle of the city's walls. The market square inside the Porta was reserved in the early medieval period as a fairground for peasants who lived in the surrounding countryside. One fair, called the *Fiera dei Contratti* (Contracts Fair), was reserved for fathers to bring their nubile daughters to be auctioned off in marriage to the highest bidder. The prospective brides walked up and down a hill to display their physical attributes while buyers bargained with the fathers over dowries. Being more refined, and disgusted by such uncouth practices, the aristocracy made their own transactions more tasteful (but just as upsetting) through negotiations between families. The chivalric code started shattering these practices. The main revolution in the code was that women were not to be seen as marriage partners, but as equal romantic partners in courtship and marriage, with the right to choose their own romantic destinies.

A classic early example of this emerging social reality is the medieval story of the love affair between Paolo and Francesca in the thirteenth century, immortalized by the Florentine poet Dante in Canto V of his *Inferno* (the first book of his *Divine Comedy*, c. 1320). Based on actual historical events, the story tells the tale of Francesca da Rimini, whose hand in marriage was promised to Giovanni Malatesta (known with the nickname of Gianciotto) to solidify the peace between warring families. Because Francesca's father suspected that she would reject the repulsive Gianciotto, he asked Gianciotto's handsome and charming younger brother, Paolo, to convince her of the necessity of the marriage pact. As it turned out, this was a mistake, since Francesca fell instantly and madly in love with the strikingly handsome Paolo, leading to a secret love affair between them. Realizing that Paolo was not going to be her spouse, and that she would be forced to marry Gianciotto, Francesca became enraged, defying her father's wishes, throwing all caution to the winds—even refusing to live without Paolo's love. According to Dante, the love was kindled after the two lovers had themselves read the story of Lancelot and Guinevere, one of first examples of chivalric love literature, indicating how significant and socially influential the chivalric code was starting to become in medieval Europe. At one point in their tryst, Gianciotto, having become jealous and suspicious, caught the two secret lovers in the act of kissing passionately. So emotionally powerful and socially subversive was this act that it influenced many subsequent stories and art works dealing with love, including Rodin's awe-inspiring *Kiss* sculpture of 1886, which portrays Paolo and Francesca in an ardent embrace that has come to symbolize romance in an enduring immutable way (Fig. 1.2):

The tragic ending comes when the jealous Gianciotto, hiding behind a curtain as the two kissed, reveals himself. He charges at his brother with a rapier. But Francesca, consumed by love, throws herself between the two brothers and the blade passes through her, killing her immediately.

Fig. 1.2   *The Kiss (Rodin, 1886)* (Wikimedia Commons)

Completely beside himself, for he desired Francesca desperately, Gianciotto then kills his brother. Paolo and Francesca were buried in the same tomb, even though they defied the marriage pact, symbolizing their union beyond mortal life.

The Paolo and Francesca story is symbolic (and historically real) of the power of love to impel people to go against traditions, no matter what the consequences may be. The story, and others like it, have left us with a picture of what love should be all about—passionate, not restrained or ordinary, and certainly not constrained by social traditions. Romantic love, sealed with a kiss, transcends both life and death, no matter what society thinks. Because of the global village in which we now live, this idealistic portrait has migrated somewhat throughout the world, finding its way into, and changing (or at least upsetting), some traditions and courtship practices. Romantic love is about the ideal, not the real. For a moment in time, it suspends the real and makes the world perfect, as depicted by Dante in his marvelous story and Rodin in his artistic masterpiece. When it works, it shatters the habitual, making us forget the trivial things that make up everyday life. Love does not obey the laws of society; it obeys those of the heart.

The murderous revenge of a love partner caught in the act of betrayal has become a common theme in contemporary narratives. The main plot of the 2002 movie *Chicago* is about fame-hungry Roxie Hart, who dreams of a successful life on the vaudeville stage, in the bright lights of Chicago, hoping to flee from her boring and dismal life with her husband Amos. Her hero is famous club singer Velma Kelly (who is in prison for murdering her own husband and sister, after discovering their affair). Roxie meets Fred Cassely, a man who convinces her that he can "make her showbiz career take off." But after Fred has gratified himself sexually (which was his real intent from the outset), Roxie realizes that she was duped, and that he has no more connections in show business than she herself does. In a rage she shoots and kills Fred. Her doting husband is, at first, prepared to take the blame for her. But after discovering her infidelity, he refuses to do so and Roxie is sentenced to jail to hang. In prison she finally meets Velma, who had become infamous for the double murder she committed. She also meets other females awaiting trial for the murders of their own partners. The movie alludes to the same theme of the Paolo and Francesca story, the Medea legend, and many others—love and its betrayal compel us to commit murderous acts of revenge. This is the central theme of the opera, *Pagliacci* (1892), by Ruggero Leoncavallo. The plot is about a Commedia dell'Arte troupe, in which the actor who plays the clown, the Pagliaccio, discovers his wife's infidelity, surreptitiously catching the lovers in the act (much like Gianciotto did). In a famous scene (*Vesti la giubba*, "Put on your costume"), the clown looks into the mirror as he puts on his make-up and clothes, ridiculing himself for being a true *pagliaccio*, as he disintegrates emotionally over the infidelity. Ironically, his skit on stage is all about that very infidelity since the actors in it are his real wife and her real lover, who play-act what they are actually doing in real life.

Divorce was an alien concept in the era of Paolo and Francesca. Certainly, it would have provided a legal, non-lethal way out of their dilemma. The bonds of marriage were seen as sacred, predestined by God, and thus as unbreakable. To quote Mark 10:2–12: "What God has joined together, let no one separate." The first act of divorce in Europe is traced to Henry VIII's marriage annulment from Catherine of Aragon so that he could marry Anne Boleyn in 1533. But the first English divorce law was passed centuries later in 1857 by the British Parliament. Divorce is now part of the love-marriage game, considered by some to be merely a stage in the game, with the term "starter marriage" now describing first-time marriages. One of the reasons indicated by statisticians for the rise in divorce rates is the economic independence of the partners. Women entered the workforce en masse in the middle part of the twentieth century, gaining control over their economic ability to decide whether or not to stay in a marriage. In this social environment, the role of romantic love as an intrinsic requirement to the success of marriage has surfaced broadly in true chivalric code style. If the marriage does not work out, divorce offers a safe exit from it.

Love and marriage still go together like a horse and carriage, as the famous 1955 Frank Sinatra song suggested, but the world is no longer as simplistic socially as it was in the past. Never before has there been such an open acceptance of open promiscuity in society at large. Nonetheless, romantic love, *à la* Paolo and Francesca, remains a social obsession. Many best-selling novels and blockbuster movies revolve around this chivalric theme. In a scene in the movie *Pretty Woman*, Julia Roberts, in the role of prostitute Vivian Ward, proclaims that she will have sex with her clients, but not kiss them, because she wants to avoid developing romantic feelings for them. As this and other movies suggest, we continue to perceive a difference between love and sex, with love entailing a deeper commitment than sexuality will allow. Yet this does not answer the fundamental conundrum of the *raison d'être* of love. Today, we still turn to our poets, composers, artists, writers, movie directors, and philosophers to unravel this enigma. But we also turn to science, for the first time in history, in the hope that science can provide an answer that is more definitive and concrete than the one provided by the artists, the philosophers, and the poets.

The Science of Love

The scientific approach to unraveling the meaning of love started with Sigmund Freud and the early behavioral psychologists, such as John B. Watson, who saw love as an innate emotion connected to childhood experiences and development. Watson observed that babies who were stimulated by certain events showed three basic emotions—fear, anger, and love.[22] These were innate, emerging in childhood in identical ways across the world. For Freud the unconscious sexual feelings developed and suppressed in childhood guided the individual's reactions to romantic stimuli at puberty and beyond.[23] Freud did not deal with romantic love as such, but rather with sexual urges as instinctive impulses. He believed that many childhood memories were shaped by sexual feelings, viewing his patients' reports of aberrant sexual experiences as fantasies reflecting unconscious desires. He theorized that sexual functioning begins at birth, and that an individual goes through several psychological stages of sexual development, which is interrupted in some people who become fixated with sex at adolescence.

Interestingly, Freud resorted to the ancient myths in order to understand human behavior. One of these was the Oedipus myth, which he believed explained the process of sexual development in its own imaginative way, claiming that in children there is hostility toward the parent of the same sex and an attraction to the parent of the opposite sex; this attraction eventually manifests itself in some neurotic behavior. He wrote about his notion in a letter to a friend[24]:

> Being entirely honest with oneself is a good exercise. Only one idea of general value has occurred to me. I have found love of the mother and jealousy of the father in my own case too, and now believe it to be a general phenomenon of early childhood. If that is the case, the gripping power of Oedipus Rex, in spite of all the rational objections to the inexorable fate that the story presupposes, becomes intelligible. Our feelings rise against any arbitrary individual fate but the Greek myth seizes on a compulsion which everyone recognizes because he has felt traces of it in himself. Every member of the audience was once a budding Oedipus in fantasy, and this dream-fulfillment played out in reality causes everyone to recoil in horror, with the full measure of repression which separates his infantile from his present state.

In order to investigate emerging psychological theories of love, in 1919, the German physician Magnus Hirschfeld opened up the first sex research institute in Berlin, which today houses an enormous library on sexual topics and which provides medical consultations to the public.[25] Hirschfeld's objective was to study the psychological reports on love and sex relations in order to gain insights into human behaviors.

Psychology was not the only discipline that turned its attention to the love and sex opposition. Beginning in the early 1930s, American anthropologist Margaret Mead and British anthropologist Bronislaw Malinowski collected data on courtship behaviors in various cultures, discovering that although the practices were culture-specific, they all seemed to share a basic pattern—a clear-cut distinction between love and sexuality.[26] Yet another early social scientist, British anthropologist Ernest Crawley, studied the role of love feelings in courtship traditions across the world, finding that the particular type of open love courtship practiced by modern urban societies is historically unique.[27]

The often-cited and controversial work of Indiana University zoologist Alfred Kinsey, which began in the late 1930s, ensconced the notion of a "science of love" once and for all. Kinsey founded the Institute for Sexual Research at the university in 1947 to study sexual practices and their implications for courtship, marriage, and even feelings of love. While teaching a marriage course, Kinsey realized that scientists had little knowledge about human sexual practices, basing most of their ideas on poetic traditions, literary writings, and even on urban legends of various types. So, he decided to take a more empirical approach, interviewing 18,500 men and women about their sexual preferences, attitudes, and overall romantic views, and then analyzing them quantitatively. These formed the basis of Kinsey's two best-selling books, *Sexual Behavior in the Human Male* (1948) and *Sexual Behavior in the Human Female* (1953), known together as the *Kinsey Report*.[28] The *Report* was controversial because people in the late 1940s and early 1950s saw its description of women as highly sexual—a taboo for the society of the era—as shocking. Even more alarming, was Kinsey's finding that many sex acts thought to be perversions at the time were so common as to be considered normal.

Since Kinsey, there has been a veritable explosion of research on the science of love, both on the part of true scientists and on the part of hucksters who peddle their books (and websites) on how to consummate love relationships successfully, reminiscent of elixir of love stories, such as the one in Gaetano Donizetti's opera, *L'elisir d'amor* (1832). The opera takes place in a village in the early 1800s. A timid youth named Nemorino is madly in love with Adina, but she is more interested in a soldier called Belcore. Nemorino buys a love potion from Dulcamara, a quack doctor, convinced that it will take effect, but it does not, as Adina adamantly intends to marry Belcore, spurning Nemorino. Nemorino joins the army and uses his enlistment money to buy another bottle of the love potion. Suddenly, he finds himself surrounded by village maidens, not because the potion is working but because (unknown to him) they found out that his rich uncle had died, leaving him a huge inheritance. A jealous Adina realizes she loves Nemorino after all and marries him. Nemorino ends up believing that it was the love potion that produced the desired result. The cagey Dulcamara makes good use of the purported "success" of the potion having customers lining up to purchase it.

A dominant theme in many genuine, not bogus, science-of-love theories is that love is a biological mechanism in "mate assessment," that allows prospective romantic partners to determine if they are suited for each other, and more importantly, if they are compatible for successful reproduction. Clinical psychologist and therapist Sue Johnson, for example, connects genetic mechanisms to mate selection.[29] She draws on the previous work of psychiatrist John Bowlby, the founder of attachment theory, who argued that we have evolved a strong, biologically-based need system in childhood that leads us to becoming attached to the mother.[30] Children carry this sense of attachment, which Johnson calls "love sense," into their adult relationships. Assessing a potential stable mate is based on improving the odds that the prospective partner possesses good genes. Beauty and physical symmetry are unconscious markers of a mate's health and genetic fitness, augmenting the love sense. In her book, *Why Him? Why Her?* Helen Fisher similarly argues that men and women use romantic strategies, such as lip kissing, in order to assess genetic compatibility and reproductive success.[31] Saliva carries genetic information, involving testosterone or estrogen (as the case may be), that is used unconsciously to assess a mate's sexual abilities and potential for fertility.

However, such theories ignore a simple Occam's razor explanation; namely that love relations tend to occur among those of similar mind or social status, or else among those who have become familiar with each other. In 2014, researchers at the University of Texas at Austin asked students to rate the physical appeal of their opposite-sex classmates.[32] The students agreed on which persons in their class were the most desirable romantically at the start of the semester. When they were asked again three months later, after spending a semester in a small class together, their judgments changed. The study concluded that evaluations of mate value change the more time people spend together. Romantic love and mate selection may in fact be different things. This has become particularly evident today, when getting onto a mobile app like Tinder, picking out a potential mate the way one would pick out an item at a store, swipe on the person's image, as if one were buying some commodity, is hardly evidence of genetically-based mate assessment. As Susan Sontag excoriated in her 1978 book of recollections, long before the Internet, love and sexual assessment do not go necessarily together[33]:

We ask everything of love. We ask it to be anarchic. We ask it to be the glue that holds the family together, that allows society to be orderly and allows all kinds of material processes to be transmitted from one generation to another. But I think that the connection between love and sex is very mysterious. Part of the modern ideology of love is to assume that love and sex always go together. They can, I suppose, but I think rather to the detriment of either one or the other. And probably the greatest problem for human beings is that they just don't. And why do people want to be in love? That's really interesting. Partly, they want to be in love the way you want to go on a roller coaster again—even knowing you're going to have your heart broken. What fascinates me about love is what it has to do with all the cultural expectations and the values that have been put into it. I've always been amazed by the people who say, "I fell in love, I was madly, passionately in love, and I had this affair." And then a lot of stuff is described and you ask, "How long did it last?" And the person will say, "A week, I just couldn't stand him or her."

Starting in 1960 and for forty-two years after, the play called *The Fantasticks* played at an off-Broadway venue. The plot was simple but wildly popular—boy meets girl; boy loses girl; boy finds her again; they fall madly in love and live happily ever after. This narrative blueprint has been an inherent one in society. It implies that, sooner or later, falling in love spontaneously (*agape*) occurs. But this is not necessarily the case. A 2015 *New York Times* essay, "To Fall in Love with Anyone, Do This," written by Mandy Len Catron, tells the story of how, feeling helpless and in a loveless rut, she turned to a famous 1997 experiment by Arthur Aron that "tried making people fall in love" with a set of 36 questions.[34] Catron and a male acquaintance repeated the experiment and ultimately came to a relevant conclusion: "We're in love because we each made the choice to be." Although the study was anecdotal, it suggests that love is hardly inevitable; it is a subjective decision. It also implies that we seek *agape*, not just enact the urges of *eros*.

The mate assessment theoretical paradigm is associated with evolutionary psychology, which sees genetic processes as generative of cultural ones.[35] Adopting Richard Dawkins' concept of *memes*, namely of units of non-genetic information that are passed on in cultural environments in order to enhance survivability and promote progress by replacing the functions of genes, the evolutionary psychologists see nothing mysterious in love.[36] It is part of a memetic process that involves no intentionality on the part of the receiving human organism, helping us simply enhance our collective ability to survive as a species. Neurohormones such as oxytocin in females and vasopressin in males are described as elements in the mate assessment mechanism, which provide unconscious information to partners about their reproductive success.

Both hormones are triggered by orgasm, and this in turn stimulates dopamine in the reward regions of the brain, impelling the mates to form an emotional bond. This engenders the feeling we call sentimentally, *love*. In most mammals, the bond lasts only as long as it takes to rear the young. In humans, this is not the case, since it can outlast the rearing period. So, love is nothing but a result of mating, not of something else. This perspective goes contrary to everything ever contemplated about love. There is evidence, however, that such a strict genetic perspective is a specious one. A study of over 500 men, conducted by a team of Swedish researchers, found that men with two copies of a specific gene scored significantly lower on a questionnaire known as the Partner Bonding Scale and reported twice as many marital crises.[37] They were also twice as likely to be involved in outside relationships and far less likely to have ever been married than those not carrying the allele. But the researchers conclude something unexpectedly: people jeopardize their family, safety, and social standing for "true love," whatever chemicals are involved. This is somewhat in contrast to the evolutionary psychology perspective. It suggests that regardless of the love chemicals, people seek love at any cost.

To paraphrase the French philosopher Michel Foucault, human beings seek to understand and define their reality by ascribing it to nature, human effort, or God.[38] As others have done in the past, mate assessment theorists have placed most of their bets on nature. Romantic behaviors are, of course, partially embedded in biology; but they are not totally so. Genetic factors alone do not completely define human love. They tell us nothing about why we experience love as a meaningful life event. The romance between Paolo and Francesca did not enhance their survival, nor did the love of all those ancient lovers who suffered tragic ends. Any true science of love would understand that neurological and chemical changes in the body are reactants to emotional states, not the triggers of what we call love, which may well reside in the human imagination and, thus, in a domain of fantasy, as the late pop artist Andy Warhol so eloquently pointed out[39]:

> Fantasy love is much better than reality love. Never doing it is very exciting. The most exciting attractions are between two opposites that never meet.

Warhol is implying that love is best when it occurs in a world of fantasy, rather than in real physical interactions. As an aside, this might explain why extramarital affairs have always been so prevalent.[40] As Shirley Glass and Thomas Wright reported in 1985, among those engaging in infidelity, 56 percent of men and 34 percent of women rated their marriage as "happy."[41] If they left a marriage, it was because they "fell in love" with someone else, leading them to fantasize about the new partner, no matter what consequences this may wreak, socially, financially, and even psychologically—a subtext captured in many previous narratives, such as by Leo Tolstoy in his novel *Anna Karenina* (1877), Boris Pasternak in *Doctor Zhivago* (1957), Vladimir Nabokov in *Lolita* (1955), and in many others.

Perhaps at no other time in history has the fantasy element in the pursuit of love become so conspicuous as in the era of cyberspace.[42] Today, love fantasies play out as much in hyperreality as they do in reality, to use a relevant term introduced by the late French philosopher and semiotician Jean Baudrillard.[43] Hyperreality refers to the world as it presents itself on the screen. The boundary between reality and hyperreality forms a *simulacrum*, a simulated mindset whereby we can no longer distinguish, or want to distinguish, between the two. Eventually, as we engage habitually with hyperreality, everything—from politics to love—becomes governed by simulation. Does this mean that romantic love is mutating into a simulacrum, whereby love with machines may constitute a means to indulge our fantasies better than we can with real bodies? Henrik Christensen of the European Research Network has claimed that people are going to be having more and more sex with robots than with humans.[44] If this is so, then Baudrillard's predictions ring disturbingly true.

But fantasy love has always been a fact of human life, not just a product of the Internet age. Federico Fellini, for example, had already satirized it in his 1976 movie, *Casanova*, in which the protagonist falls in love with a mechanical doll, which he prefers to a real life woman. It seems that "fantasy love" can lead, sometimes, to "fetish love." The term fetish referred originally to an inanimate object believed to be imbued with supernatural attributes. The term was recycled by Sigmund Freud to describe sexual urges and fantasies that persistently involve the use of objects by themselves or, at times, with a sexual partner.[45] When we experience an abundance of sexual energy, which is suppressed because of social constraints, we might easily become enmeshed in a form of fetishistic fantasy love, as an outlet for the suppressions.

Opposition and Continuum Theory

Outside of Roland Barthes, who compiled a list of aphorisms about love from philosophy and literature (mentioned in the preface), no semiotician has considered looking at love as a meaning-making force in human life, at least to the best of my knowledge.[46] Whatever the reason for this neglect, it is saliently obvious that the topic of love is an important one, cognitively and culturally, having been semiotized since antiquity in the form of myths, stories, art works, etc.

There are two general principles that are useful for examining love semiotically, since they complement each other. One is a consideration of how love and sex form an *opposition* and how this informs the representations of the two notions in various media, from writing to art; the other is the notion that interactions among the body, mind, and culture form a semiotic continuum, with each one interconnected with the other two, thus asserting that love, sex, and cultural codes of romance and gender are inextricably intertwined. An opposition in semiotics, as pointed out in the preface, does not imply that two concepts are opposite ones in the usual understanding of this term, although this may be true in some cases. Love is not the opposite of sex; it is its correlative notion—that is, we understand one in terms of the other through the differential representations we have developed to encode them (different words, symbols, texts, etc.). This implies that we sense intuitively that both exist as psychic forces directing human life and are thus interconnected in some inherent way. For this reason, we perceive them as forming a meaningful opposition—one entails the other differentially. All signs and sign systems bear meaning in relation to other signs and systems in specific contexts. We also understand *love* in terms of its true semantic opposite *hate*, but this type of opposition produces a different meaning constellation. The story of Medea, for example, shows how the betrayal of love leads to hate and how this, in turn, induces revenge and its destructive consequences. In the story, love and hate are entangled in an intricate web of emotions that direct human actions. The story of Cupid, on the other hand, deals arguably with the tug of emotional war that exists between love and sexuality, which involves a different semiotic dynamic than the love-hate one evident in the Medea story. In sum, the parts of an opposition form a semiotic unit—one cannot exist without the other. An analogy is useful. In a simple physical system, such as the *on-off* one of alarm systems, we understand each state in terms of the other, constituting a feedback loop—a ringing alarm signal carries different information than one that is silent because the latter is the expected state of the alarm system and the former its alerting state. When an alarm is tripped in some way, the feedback process is started and the information load of the system increases. This type of oppositional structure exists in human emotional and cognitive systems in a similar way. In other words, an opposition is a semiotic feedback loop system that informs us about the elements in the system as they relate to one another.

For the sake of historical accuracy, it should be mentioned that opposition theory has roots in antiquity, where it was called dualism. Aristotle, for instance,

developed his philosophical system on the basis of a set of existential oppositions: unity-multiplicity, being-nothingness, and others.[47] The oppositional
nature of the love-sex (and love-hate) dualism surfaces in the ancient texts of
cultures across the world, as we have seen, acknowledging that people across
time and cultural spaces have ascribed significance to this inner dynamic in
similar ways. The earliest use of opposition theory within semiotics proper is
found in the *Cours de linguistique générale*, by Ferdinand de Saussure, the
nineteenth-century founder of the discipline.[48] As an example of how a single
opposition is encoded in various systems, with each system looping on the
other, consider the *left-right* one. This is derived, arguably, from the fact that
we have a left hand (and foot, leg, ear, and eye) and a right one. Now, this
physically-based opposition is encoded at different levels of representation,
generating specific cultural oppositions. *Right* is associated with *good* and *left*
with *evil* (the word *sinister* derives from Latin *sinistra* "on the left, unlucky.")
It crystallizes in artistic religious representations, as can be seen in the fresco
of the *Last Judgment* painted by Michelangelo in the ceiling of the Sistine
Chapel, in which Christ is depicted as condemning evil sinners to hell with
his left hand but permitting passage to heaven for good people with a blessing
of his right hand. The word *right* is used commonly in English-speaking societies (and others) to convey concepts of "correctness," "truth," "justice." In the
United States, *The Bill of Rights* is a legal document that lays out the *rights* to
which each person is entitled. The list of the manifestations of the right-left
opposition is a huge one. It creates a network of interrelated meanings that
constitute a portion of a culture. Nature makes no social, artistic, or other
semiotically-based distinctions between right and left; people do.

As a semiotic technique, opposition theory was elaborated by a number of
linguists who met regularly in Prague in the early 1920s, using it to examine
how we extract meaning from language forms. Psychologist Charles Ogden
claimed at about the same time that "the theory of opposition offers a new
method of approach not only in the case of all those words which can best be
defined in terms of their opposites, or of the oppositional scale on which they
appear, but also to any word."[49] As Ogden also demonstrated, there are
gradations within oppositions themselves. For example, between *night* and
day there is *dawn, noon, twilight*, and other gradations in English culture. So
too between *love* and *sex* there are conceptual gradations indicated by words
such as *intimacy, romance, affection, eroticism, sensuality*, some of which are
closer in cognitive space to *love* and others to *sex*.

A second principle that can be used to consider love semiotically is (as mentioned above) the concept that the body, the mind, and environment (or culture) form a semiotic continuum. In this approach, *sex* would be located in

the *body* sector of the continuum, constituting what American philosopher Charles Sanders Peirce called a "Firstness" phenomenon, an instinctive, yet meaning-based, reaction to something that occurs at the level of the body.[50] From this initial state, centered on the body's sensory and instinctual system, sexual feelings are projected onto an emotional sector of the continuum, which corresponds to what we call *love*. Love, in Peircean terms, is a "Secondness" relation—a relation that occurs in response to, and in tandem with, bodily processes. Finally, the ways in which we represent love and sex in cultural ways (through language, art, myths, etc.) constitutes a "Thirdness" relation, falling on another part of the continuum. This may sound somewhat obscure, but it is actually a rather insightful way of alluding to the interconnection between the body, the mind, and the world. A similar paradigm comes from British philosopher Karl Popper, which is worth considering here schematically since it provides a concrete way of visualizing the semiotic continuum.[51]

Popper classifies the ways in which we process and utilize information into three domains. "World 1" is how we initially respond to physical information (objects and states) stimulating neuronal synapses that transmit messages along nerve paths that cause muscles to contract or limbs to move. "World 2" is the domain of the subjective interpretation of the same information, shaped by upbringing and individual propensities. "World 3" is the domain of culturally-based models of the same information. World 1 is the pre-conscious domain of the instincts and sense impressions. Sex is a World 1 state. World 2 is anchored in the imagination and in Self-evaluations of inner feelings. This is where love emerges as a blend of instincts and feelings. And World 3 coincides with representations, definitions, rituals, etc. connected to love, sex, and their derivative constructs (gender, courtship, etc.). It is at this level that love practices and traditions such as marriage occur. Again, the three levels are not mutually exclusive; they are part of a continuum of interactive meanings. This is arguably why love betrayals outside of marriage have been seen traditionally as disrupting the sensed fluidity that should exist between the three cognitive domains and thus as an act of violation of the unity of love with the body and the world. The early stories about betrayals, elopements, and the like are evidence that we have been obsessed by our acts of violation of this continuum, how they affect us adversely, and what they tell us about the human condition generally.

The continuum notion also allows us to grasp the meanings of gender in semiotic-cultural terms. The concepts of *male* and *female* form an opposition at the physical (World 1) level, referring to the primary sexual differences that biology imposes on organisms. *Masculinity* and *femininity*, on the other hand, are correlative gender concepts, constituting products of both Worlds 2 and 3. Every culture develops its own particular canons of morality and lifestyle that largely determine the choices individuals make throughout their lives. Gender is one of those canons. It is not part of nature, but of human convention. A subtext of this book is that love transcends sexuality and is blind to gender codes. It is a feeling shared by humans of all genders and sexual orientations, rendering such notions moot.

In effect, across the world, views of what is *natural* in matters of sex and gender are established by tradition and consensus. This is why they vary across the world. In the traditional culture of the Etoro peoples of New Guinea, for example, there exists an intense distaste for heterosexual relations, because the denizens of that culture believe that these shorten life.[52] Etoro custom discourages such relations for more than 200 days out of the year, restricting them by and large to ensuring reproduction. Homosexual relations, on the other hand, are praised and encouraged; romance is seen as connected to these. The same kind of perception exists among the traditional Chukchee peoples of Siberia. Chukchee males can become powerful social figures only if they engage in sexual relations with other males. Western society, on the other hand, has responded ambiguously towards diverse gender systems.[53] In ancient Greece, homosexual relations were permitted, and, in some cases, even expected among certain social classes. However, attitudes towards diverse sexualities and gender identities were overwhelmingly negative in western culture until the middle part of the twentieth century, as individuals in all walks of life, growing up in all kinds of families, practicing many different religions, became open about their diverse sexualities and gender identities. Since then studies on the relation between gender and sexuality have become common. For example, a 2014 study by Manago, Greenfield, Kim, and Ward showed that in a society where free choice in matters of love and sex exists, so too do perceptions of gender identity become more flexible and tolerant.[54] Another relevant study by Baumeister and Mondoza linked the acceptance of sexual diversity with gender equality.[55] The researchers designed their study to test the theory that sexual norms and practices are more restrictive in areas where gender inequality reigns as a social construct. Using an international online sex survey involving 37 nations the researchers found that gender equality was associated with more casual sex, more sexual partners per capita, younger ages for first sex, and greater tolerance of premarital sex.

The semiotic opposition between sex and love, and the meaning-making continuum among love, sex, and culture, cannot be defined in purely scientific terms. This does not deny the existence of events and states in the body that will lead to a feeling shared universally, as the narratives and representational traditions across cultures have saliently shown. All organisms have a species-specific bodily alerting system that informs them of emotional changes in their bodies. But these are interpreted in culture-specific ways. Moreover, in love and courtship rituals, the presentation of the Self (World 2) is shaped by culture (World 3). Since the beginning of time we have envisioned culture-specific models of attractiveness as part of the Self-presentation game in courtship. This is why facial decorations and alterations constitute beauty-enhancing props that reach back into the origins of culture. Red lipstick, for example, is perceived in many cultures to connote the redness associated with female fertility; the wearing of mustaches or beards by males connotes virility in others. From the beginning of time, human beings have made up their faces to convey gender identity as well as images of attractiveness, in order to stimulate the love feeling. As anthropologist Helen Fisher has aptly remarked, the sexually-constructed face is a characteristic Self-representational phenomenon that reaches back to our Cro-Magnon ancestors, who spent hours decorating themselves, plaiting their hair, and donning garlands of flowers to show off for one another around the fire's glow.[56] The contemporary cosmetic and jewelry industries are modern-day versions of these age-old traditions.

Interestingly, psychologists have found that specific individuals are responsive romantically to certain kinds of faces and not to others from puberty onwards. One explanation as to why such preferences surface at puberty is the presence of what the psychologist John Money calls "lovemaps" in the mind.[57] He defines these as mental images that determine the specific kinds of features of the face that will evoke sexual arousal and love moods (such as infatuation) in an individual. Lovemaps are developed during childhood in response to various environmental experiences and influences. At adolescence, they unconsciously generate an image of what the ideal "sweetheart" should be like, becoming quite specific as to details of the physiognomy of the ideal lover, as well as to the general demeanor of the prospective paramour.

Epilogue

To summarize the main argument put forward in this chapter, the connection between love, sex, gender, courtship practices, and marriage is forged through meaning-making structures (opposition and continuum theory) that are involved in unconsciously uniting the body, mind, and environment. So, notions of love result from the shared experiences of people in different areas of the world and in different eras of time. There are some constants, nonetheless. People the world over have always conceptualized love as distinct for sexuality, although somehow connected to it. We have traditionally married for practical or social reasons, as part of negotiations between families, for political motives, and so on. Marriage became based on love and romance, as argued here, because of the chivalric code, conceding to love on the continuum as the dominant force. As a consequence, betrayals, affairs, and break-ups surged among common folk, not just among heroes and gods as in the ancient myths. It is the possibility of choice, which comes with free love, that is both the upside and the downside of love. What this means for the future of marriage and even the concept of family will be entertained in the final chapter.

Stories such as the Romeo and Juliet one were early idealized framings of the chivalric perception of love as a liberating force from the yoke of traditions. The story may actually recount a true historical event. Some medieval scholars and literary historians place the origin of the story in the late 1200s or early 1300s. It was Shakespeare, of course, who made it famous, shaping it into a romantic narrative that has subsequently shaped all such stories. Shakespeare's rendition was published in quarto in 1597. It was his first tragedy; and it is significant that he dealt with the idealism of youthful love and its oppositional connection with hate and death. To the two star-crossed lovers, love is both frightening and blissful; through love they rise to heroism and become noble in their humanity. Shakespeare probably based his tale on a 1562 narrative poem by Arthur Brooke, *The Tragical History of Romeo and Juliet*, which was a translation and adaptation of *Giulietta e Romeo* by the Italian Matteo Bandello. The earliest written version of the tale dates back to a 1476 story, by Masuccio Salernitano, in his collection called *Il Novellino*. It is in the fateful Act V of Shakespeare's play that, upon hearing of Juliet's death, which unbeknownst to Romeo is faked, the star-crossed lover drinks poison in front of his beloved, kissing her and uttering his final words: "Thus with a kiss I die." The Shakespearean tale is an idealistic and powerful adaptation of previous texts—a process of semiotic transmission that is technically called *interextuality*, that is, one text informing another over time.

Shakespeare may have also been inspired by the Paolo and Francesca story or even by the legendary twelfth-century love tryst between Peter Abelard and Héloïse. Abelard, a theologian, began tutoring Héloïse, the niece of a canon of the Cathedral of Notre-Dame in Paris, in 1117. They fell in love and secretly married after Héloïse gave birth to a son. Abelard then persuaded his paramour to take holy vows. Believing that Abelard had abandoned Héloïse, her uncle had him castrated. In response, Abelard founded a chapel called the Paraclete, where Héloïse became abbess. In 1125, he became abbot of the monastery at Saint-Gildas-de-Rhuis. A little later the two lovers began their famous correspondence, which became a model of romantic language. Upon his death, Abelard's body was taken to the Paraclete; and when Héloïse died she was buried beside him. Their bodies now lie in a single tomb in the Père Lachaise cemetery in Paris. In his autobiography, *The Story of My Misfortunes*, Abelard indicates that he dreamt of loving Héloïse long before he had the opportunity to do so.

Countless stories have since been written about the idealism of young lovers whose parents disapprove of their romance, recalling Shakespeare's play and the stories of other star-crossed lovers. These have become ingrained in our cultural DNA. To reiterate here, love is an ideal; it is part of the way we wish to fantasize about those to whom we are strongly attracted, as Andy Warhol so aptly pointed out. When it works, it shatters the habitual, makes us forget mundane arguments, jealousies, and all the other hassles that make up the banality of everyday life. As social critic Emma Goldman, wrote: "Rather would I have the love songs of romantic ages, rather Don Juan and Madame Venus, rather an elopement by ladder and rope on a moonlight night, followed by the father's curse, mother's moans, and the moral comments of neighbors, than correctness and propriety measured by yardsticks."[58]

However, as the ancient Greek philosophers understood, love can become obsession. For this reason, we have developed strategies throughout time to tame it in some concrete way. There is an intriguing modern-day story that brings this out anecdotally. A 2015 *U.S. News* article by journalist Jo Craven McGinty summarizes the relevant situation as follows[59]:

A few years ago, a lonely American in London began to ponder his chances of finding a girlfriend. Surely in a city of eight million people, plenty of women would find a dark-haired doctoral candidate in economics attractive. But just how many women might be into him? What were his actual odds of finding love?

McGinty goes on to explain that the "dark-haired doctoral candidate," who was thirty-one at the time, used the Drake equation to identify the number of women who might be amorously interested in him. The result was a meager twenty-six. The Drake equation was devised by scientist Frank Drake in 1961 to estimate the number of planets in our galaxy purportedly able to sustain intelligent life. McGinty explains how this formula, modified accordingly, was applied by the doctoral candidate to romance:

In a given population—say, London or New York or wherever you happen to live—you apply a series of increasingly restrictive criteria until you end up with a subpopulation that satisfies all the conditions…Of course, statistics aren't available for every characteristic, and increasing the number of conditions—being choosier, if you will—quickly shrinks the pool of prospective mates.

McGinty points out that the formula for a young man living, say, in Philadelphia, produces 171 individuals who fit it. Of course, if true, finding them is another story. This mathematical anecdote has even penetrated popular culture. It was used, for example, in an episode of *The Big Bang Theory* where the nerdy protagonists applied it to estimating their hook-up odds on "anything can happen Thursday." Their use of the formula might, of course, be seen as their rationalization for *not* finding a mate, using mathematics in lieu of obtaining love. McGinty concludes that the thirty-one-year-old "found and married someone who matched his parameters." In the end, all this shows is the extent to which we will go to achieve romance, attempting to tame it at a rational level.

Notes

1. See Michael Allen and Valery Rees, *Marsilio Ficino: His Theology, His Philosophy, His Legacy* (Leiden: Brill, 2002).
2. Charles Darwin, *The Origin of Species* (New York: Collier).
3. Jane Goodall, *In the Shadow of Man* (Boston: Mariner Books, 1971), p. 29.
4. Jakob von Uexküll, *Umwelt und Innenwelt der Tierre* (Berlin: Springer, 1909).
5. Erich Fromm, *The Art of Loving* (New York: Harper, 1956).
6. D. H. Lawrence, *Studies in Classic American Literature* (Cambridge: Cambridge University Press, 1923), p. 57.
7. See Empedocles, *The Fragments of Empedocles*, ed. by William Ellery (Marrickville: Wentworth Press, 2016).
8. Plato, *Symposium* (London: Macmillan, 1892).
9. Jennifer Wright Knust, *Unprotected Texts: The Bible's Surprising Contradictions About Sex and Desire* (New York: HarperOne, 2011).
10. Michael Coogan, *God and Sex: What the Bible Really Says* (New York: Twelve, 2010). See also Edward Ackerley, *The X-Rated Bible: An Irreverent Survey of Sex in Scripture* (New York: feral House, 1999); Philo Telos, *Divine Sex: Liberating Sex from Religious Tradition* (New York: Trafford, 2006); Teresa Hornsby, *Sex Texts from the Bible: Selections Annotated & Explained* (New York: Skylight Paths); and Darrel Ray, *Sex & God: How Religion Distorts Sexuality* (New York: IPC Press, 2012).
11. Apollonius Rhodius, *Argonautica*, Book 3, translated by Seaton, R. C. Loeb (London, William Heinemann Ltd, 1912), p. 947.
12. In Maurice Balme and James Morewood, *Oxford Latin Reader* (Oxford: Oxford University Press, 1997).

13. Lucretius, *De rerum natura* (New York: Loeb Classical Library, 1975).

14. Ovid, *Ars Amatoria* (New York: Kessinger, 2004).

15. Sheril Kirshenbaum, *The Science of Kissing: What Our Lips Are Telling Us* (New York: Grand Central, 2011), p. 40.

16. For a historiography of theories and views on the kiss, see Adrianne Blue, *On Kissing: From the Metaphysical to the Erotic* (London: Victor Gollancz, 1996).

17. Kirshenbaum, *The Science of Kissing*, pp. 41–42.

18. The cave is described by Plato in his *Republic*—see Plato, *The Republic*, ed. by C. D. C. Reeve (Indianapolis: Hackett, 2004).

19. An in-depth account of the historical background to chivalry is the one by Hywell Williams, *The Age of Chivalry: Culture and Power in Medieval Europe 950–1450* (London: Quercus, 2011).

20. Andreas Capellanus, *The Art of Courtly Love*, Trans. by J. J. Perry (New York: Columbia University Press, 1941).

21. Giovanni Pico della Mirandola, *Commentary on a Love Song of Girolamo Benivieni* (Baltimore: John Hopkins University Press, 1967), p. 126.

22. John B. Watson, *Psychology from the Standpoint if a Behaviorist* (Philadelphia: Lippincott, 1919).

23. Sigmund Freud, *Sexuality and the Psychology of Love* (New York: Simon and Schuster 1997).

24. Cited in Martin Grotjahn, *Beyond Laughter: Humor and the Subconscious* (New York: McGraw-Hill, 1966), p. 84.

25. Magnus Hirschfeld, *Men and Women: The World Journey of a Sexologist* (New York: AMS Press, 1933).

26. Bronislaw Malinowski, *Sex and Repression in Savage Society* (London: Routledge & Kegan Paul, 1927), Margaret Mead, *Sex and Temperament in Three Primitive Societies* (New York: Perennial, 1936).

27. Ernest Crawley, *Primitive Marriage and Its System* (Kila, Montana: Kessinger Publications Reprint, 2005).

28. Alfred Kinsey, *Sexual Behavior in the Human Male* (Bloomington: Indiana University Press, 1948), and *Sexual Behavior in the Human Female* (Bloomington: Indiana University Press, 1953).

29. Sue Johnson, *Love Sense: The Revolutionary New Science of Romantic Relationships* (New York: Little, Brown, and Co., 2013), p. 12.

30. For example, John Bowlby, *The Making and Breaking of Affectional Bonds* (London: Routledge, 1979).

31. Helen Fisher, *Why Him? Why Her? Finding Real Love by Understanding Your Personality Type* (New York: Macmillan, 2009).

32. Paul W. Eastwick and Lucy L. Hunt, "Relational Mate Vale: Consensus and Uniqueness in Romantic Evaluations," *Journal of Personal and Social Psychology* 106: 728–251.

33. Cited in Susan Sontag, *Susan Sontag: The Complete Rolling Stone Interview* (New Haven: Yale University Press, 2013).

34. Mandy Len Catron, "To Fall in Love with Anyone, Do This," *New York Times*, 2015, https://www.nytimes.com/2015/01/11/fashion/modern-love-to-fall-in-love-with-anyone-do-this.html.

35. See David M. Buss, *Evolutionary Psychology: The New Science of the Mind* (Boston: Pearson, 2004) for an overview.

36. Richard Dawkins, *The Selfish Gene* (Oxford: Oxford University Press, 1976).

37. H. Walum, L. Westberg, S. Henningsson, J. M. Neiderhiser, D. Reiss, W. Igl, J. M. Ganiban, E. L. Spotts, N. L. Pedersen, E. Eriksson, and P. Lichtenstein, "Genetic Variation in the Vasopressin Receptor 1a Gene (AVPR1A) Associates with Pair-Bonding Behavior in Humans," *Proceedings of the National Academy of Sciences* 105 (2008): 14153–14156.

38. Michel Foucault, *The Archeology of Knowledge*, trans. by A. M. Sheridan Smith (New York: Pantheon, 1972).

39. Cited in Andy Warhol, *The Philosophy of Andy Warhol: From A to B and Back Again* (Boston: Mariner Books, 1977).

40. See, for example, Joan D. Atwood and Limor Schwartz, "Cyber-Sex: The New Affair Treatment Considerations," *Journal of Couple & Relationship Therapy* 1 (2002): 37–56.

41. Shirley P. Glass and Thomas L. Wright, "Sex Differences in Type of Extramarital Involvement and Marital Dissatisfaction," *Sex Roles* 12 (1985): 1101–1119.

42. Sheril Kirshenbaum, *The Science of Kissing: What Our Lips Are Telling Us* (New York: Grand Central, 2011), p. 59.

43. Jean Baudrillard, *Simulations* (New York: Semiotexte, 1983).

44. Anthony Rust, "Sexbots: The Future, Whether You Like It or Not," *Sunday Times* January 25, 2015.

45. Sigmund Freud, "On Fetishism", in *Miscellaneous Papers, 1888–1938*, Vol. 5 of *Collected Papers* (London: Hogarth and Institute of Psycho-Analysis, 1924–1959), pp. 198–204.

46. Roland Barthes, *A Lover's Discourse: Fragments* (New York: Farrar, Straus and Giroux, 1977).

47. In Aristotle, *Metaphysics*, trans. by Montgomery Furth (Indianapolis: Hackett Publishing Company, 1985).

48. Ferdinand de Saussure, *Cours de linguistique générale* (Paris: Payot, 1916).

49. Charles K. Ogden, *Opposition: A Linguistic and Psychological Analysis* (London: Paul, Trench, and Trubner, 1932), p. 18.

50. Charles S. Peirce, *Collected Papers of Charles Sanders Peirce*, Vols. 1–8, ed. by C. Hartshorne and P. Weiss (Cambridge, Mass.: Harvard University Press, 1931–1958).

51. Karl Popper, *The Unending Quest* (Glasgow: Collins, 1976); Karl Popper and James Eccles, *The Self and the Brain* (Berlin: Springer, 1977).

52. For an overall description of diverse sexual practices, see, for instance, Robert Endleman, "Homosexuality in Tribal Societies," *Transcultural Psychiatry* 23 (1986): 187–218.

53. See F. M. Mondimore, *A Natural History of Homosexuality* (Baltimore: Johns Hopkins University Press, 1996).

54. Adriana M. Manago, Patricia M. Greenfield, and Janna L. Kim, "Changing Cultural Pathways through Gender Role and Sexual Development: A Theoretical Framework," *Ethos* 42: 198–221.

55. Roy F. Abumesiter and Juan Pablo Mendoza, "Cultural Variations in the Sexual Marketplace: Gender Equality Correlates With More Sexual Activity," *Journal of Social Psychology* 151 (2013): 350–360.

56. Helen Fisher, *Anatomy of Love* (New York: Norton, 1992), pp. 272–273.

57. John Money, *Lovemaps: Clinical Concepts of Sexual/Erotic Health and Pathology, Paraphilia, and Gender Identity from Conception to Maturity* (Baltimore: Johns Hopkins University Press, 1986).

58. Emma Goldman, *Anarchism and Other Essays* (London: Fifield, 1910), p. 23.

59. Jo Craven McGinty, "To Find a Romantic Match, Try Some Love Math," *U.S. News*, February, 2015, pp. 14–15, section A2.

2

The Body in Love

For male and female alike, the bodies of the other sex are messages signaling what
we must do—they are glowing signifiers of our own necessities.
—John Updike (1932–2009)

Prologue

Love changes the body, altering its biology and neurochemistry radically. When the first romantic lip-kiss is performed by two people who are strongly attracted to each other, there is an unmistakable adrenalin and blood rush that takes over all the other organic functions momentarily, suspending them as if they were outside the body.[1] Over time the rush might diminish, but its mnemonic residues will never dissipate—this is why we remember our first kiss and our first love years after moving on in life, and even after entering into a love relationship with someone else. Adrenalin, serotonin, dopamine and endorphins are activated in all physical acts of love, such as kissing, holding hands, and hugging. These behaviors activate the body's response system shaping facial expressions, postures, and eye contact patterns that characterize love-based situations. Semiotically, they are physical manifestation of how the body-mind-culture continuum is affected by the emotional power of love.

The expression "body-in-love" is used in an intentionally ambiguous way in this chapter. It is employed to mean the effects on the body that are engendered by love feelings, how the body contributes to effectuating these feelings, and what our semiotic representations of the body-in-love (such as portraits and clothing) tell us about our perceptions of love itself. The branch of semi-

© The Author(s) 2019
M. Danesi, *The Semiotics of Love*, Semiotics and Popular Culture,
https://doi.org/10.1007/978-3-030-18111-6_2

otics that looks at bodily signs and signals, known as nonverbal semiotics, is a highly relevant one, therefore, for understanding the love-sex opposition and its role on the semiotic continuum (previous chapter). We convey over two-thirds of our messages through the body, utilizing thousands of physical signs—postures, gestures, facial expressions, and so on.[2] The body is, in a phrase, a primary source for decoding the physical and psychological effects of love and, thus, for gaining relevant insights into its overall meaning, including the *raison d'être* of our cultural interventions, such as the use of cosmetics, grooming codes, and specific types of clothing to enhance the romantic persona. If any of the codes are violated in amorous contexts, the chances of romantic success are virtually nil—for instance, if an individual decides to wear inappropriate clothes for a romantic encounter, the potential mate might become uneasy and even interpret the choice of clothing as conflictual.

The nonverbal behaviors connected with love seem "natural" because they are acquired unreflectively in context. As discussed in the opening chapter, throughout the world certain behaviors are perceived as constituting appropriate manifestations of male and female sexuality. These are the result of gender codes that define sexuality within a tribe or society. As such, they guide the presentation of the sexual persona in public. Today, the codes have been extended considerably to include diverse sexual orientations. But throughout time, as our stories certainly have documented, we have perceived love as transcending the very codes we have devised, projecting love as a sacred force that rises above them all.[3] It should be mentioned that today, this mindset may be mutating somewhat, since we live in a simulacrum that makes it difficult to distinguish between virtual bodies (bodies represented on screens) and real bodies. This is having concrete implications for the enactment and perception of love. The three-part semiotic continuum involving the body, the mind, and culture (Worlds 1, 2, and 3) is becoming more and more susceptible to including a fourth part—the virtual hyperreal body. The implications of this development in human emotional-cognitive-social evolution will be broached subsequently.

The Face in Love

Facial expressions in human beings constitute a nonverbal sign system that is connected to the plastic musculature of the face. In 1963, psychologist Paul Ekman founded the Human Interaction Laboratory in the Department of Psychiatry at the University of California at San Francisco for the purpose of studying this system. He was joined by Wallace V. Friesen in 1965 and Maureen O'Sullivan in 1974. Over the years, Ekman and his team have established that some facial expressions are interpreted universally as signs of specific emotions, while others are shaped by cultural context.[4] They have shown this by breaking down facial musculature into characteristic components—eyebrow position, eye shape, mouth shape, nostril size, etc.—which in various combinations determine the form of the relevant *microexpressions*, as Ekman termed specific facial signs, and their interpretation. Ekman found little cross-cultural variation in the microexpressions prompted by the basic emotions—anger, fear, disgust, happiness, sadness, surprise, contempt. However, he discovered that many other kinds of microexpressions showed dissimilarity, being shaped by cultural codes of specific kinds.

Interest in facial expressions as part of courtship displays started with Charles Darwin's 1872 book *Expression of the Emotions in Man and Animals*.[5] Prior to Darwin, the face was a subject of interest mainly to visual artists as a means to portray human character and personality in a painting or a sculpture. Darwin's biological approach led gradually to the ethnographic and scientific study of facial expressions characteristic of everyday nonverbal communication. In 1964, anthropologist Margaret Mead studied isolated communities, discovering that facial expressions were, by and large, culturally-coded.[6] She noted, for example, how pubescent males and females put on different facial poses that were expected of them by their elders for reasons of courtship. At about the same time that Mead was conducting her anthropological research, psychologist Silvan Tomkins also found that most facial expressions (outside of the basic ones) are conditioned by, and learned in, social context.[7] Similar work followed in both anthropology and psychology, most of which has bolstered Ekman's findings that many microexpressions are variable, yet retain a physical essence. One of these was the face-in-love, as it can be called. In other words, while specific love-based microexpressions may vary somewhat, they result from the same "emotional complex" that characterizes the love-sex opposition. This complex has been the subject not only of scientists and portrait artists, but also of caricaturists, comic book creators, and even Unicode's creators of emoji figures.[8] The three emoji below are cases-in-point (Fig. 2.1):

Fig. 2.1 *Romance emoji*

In a light-hearted and humorous way, each one conveys a different romantic mood or intent, showing how the semiotic nuances of the love-sex opposition can be portrayed even in a comedic pictographic medium. The emoji to the left, with its "heart eyes" and contented smile, communicates a simple sense of romantic love, usually associated with the "infatuated face"; the middle one adds flirtation to the love-face, suggested not by hearts but by eyes that two people in love might use to look at each other affectionately; and the one to the right, also without heart symbols, shows a flirtatious winking face, with a wry sense of playful romantic involvement through an impish smile. These emoji impart a cheery tone to a romantic message, thus alleviating the risk of conveying vulgarity or lewdness. Even the middle and right ones transmit suggestive sexuality in an amusing and thus relatively innocuous way. The point here is that they portray the various nuances of the face-in-love in a contemporary pictographic way.

Facial expressions dovetail with eye contact patterns during courtship and flirtation situations. Like other species, humans perceive a direct stare as a threat or challenge and, like dogs and primates, will break eye contact as a signal of surrender. Most other eye contact behaviors are, however, shaped by culture, not nature, including patterns that characterize romantic and courtship situations.[9] The length of time involved in eye contact during flirtation, for example, conveys what kinds of romantic relationship people have, or wish to have, with each other in contextualized ways; people in some cultures will tend to look more into each other's eyes during romance, while in others, the paramours tend to avoid eye contact entirely for reasons of deference and respect; in other cultures still, the partners are not expected to look into each other's eyes unless they are married, in contrast to the images of "looking into each other's eyes" that Hollywood-style imagery has ensconced into groupthink. Also involved in the conveyance of romantic feelings during flirtatious eye contact is head movement.[10] It has been found, for example, that the "head tilt" position is usually assumed to convey interest in the partner, whereas the "head down" position signals a negative or judgmental attitude, with the two thus forming a semiotic opposition.[11]

Before the advent of the various scientific studies of facial expressions, visual artists were the ones who portrayed facial poses and features as indicative of the character behind the face and of insinuations of love or desire. One of these is the smile and the seductive and compelling spell it can cast over us, connecting desire and love, the body and the mind, at once. As art curator Angus Trumble has written in his history of the smile, it always "begins with an instantaneous chemical reaction, activating through certain nerves the muscles of the face, and may give to the wearer the power of wordless communication."[12] Given its emotional power, the smile has been portrayed artistically by countless painters and sculptors. Perhaps the one that best captures the intrigue, flirtatiousness, provocativeness, and mischievousness of this uniquely human microexpression is Leonardo Da Vinci's masterwork the *Mona Lisa* (known more properly as *La gioconda* in Italian, meaning "the playful one") (Fig. 2.2):

Much has been read into that enigmatic smile. According to a computer analysis conducted at the University of Amsterdam in 2006, Mona Lisa's smile indicates that she is 83 percent happy, 9 percent disgusted, 6 percent fearful, and 2 percent angry.[13] But artificial intelligence clearly cannot grasp the subtleties of flirtation imprinted in that smile, as well as its promise of sexual excitement, recalling in visual form the medieval stories of betrayal and seduction. These interpretations are embedded in historical memory, not in any algorithm. Mona Lisa's face is, in a phrase, a portrait of the face-in-love and the face-in-seductive-mode. Semioticians refer to the ways in which something is constructed to resemble some referent as iconicity—a technical term which indicates, in this case, that an artist has attempted to capture the love

Fig. 2.2 *Mona Lisa (Leonardo Da Vinci, 1503–1506)* (Wikimedia Commons)

and desire feeling states as they shape the physiology of facial expression through verisimilitude. It is Da Vinci's masterful interpretation of how someone's face both reacts to feelings and then utilizes them strategically for romantic and seductive purposes.

The look of seduction that is evident in Mona Lisa's gaze protrudes a sense of something tempting, sultry, and coquettish at once. Is this an infatuated face or a face of seduction, or both? It is this uncertainty that mirrors the ambiguity of the love-sex opposition, captured brilliantly by a master artist. Another well-known portrait that represents the face iconically is John William Waterhouse's enigmatic and suggestive painting, *Hylas and the Nymphs* (1869) (Fig. 2.3).

The enticing looks on the faces and in the eyes of the water nymphs, which are not as coy and flirtatious as in the Mona Lisa painting, are nonetheless alluring. The painting depicts the tragic legend of young Hylas of Greek and Roman mythology, who was abducted by the nymphs for sexual purposes, while he sought water. The looks on the nymphs are exemplars of what we have come to interpret as constituting a seductive face through iconicity. The faraway and distracted gazes suggest that the nymphs may be daydreaming or mesmerized by the power of love. This very same kind of "nymphal face" is common in contemporary advertising, especially in the area of cosmetics, influencing our perceptions of attractiveness. Interestingly, in Europe during

Fig. 2.3 *Hylas and the Nymphs (John William Waterhouse, 1869)* (Wikimedia Commons)

the 1930s and 1940s, extracts of the drug *belladonna* were used to sexualize the face, given that it produces extreme dilation of the pupils. Apparently, we tend to interpret a face with dilated eyes as beautiful and alluring. This drug is no longer sold as a cosmetic; it is used mainly by optometrists to facilitate eye examinations. But its cosmetic history explains the origin of its colloquial name, which in Italian means "beautiful woman."

As paintings such as the ones above illustrate, our perceptions of the face-in-love overlap considerably with our perceptions of the face-in-lust. This may be the reason why, as Debbie Nathan has pointed out, the history of erotic representations overlaps considerably with the history of romantic ones.[14] Ancient pictographs of spirits and sacred animals have been found along with those of phalluses and vessels on the same walls. Fertility rites were practiced and performed along the Tigris and Euphrates Rivers, as Herodotus noted in his *Historia*, to celebrate the sexual body, while acknowledging its sacred nature at the same time through ritualization.[15] British anthropologist James Frazer was perhaps the first to study such rites systematically in his book, *The Golden Bough*.[16] Frazer differentiated between sexual passage rites and lifelong rites, which involve a constant performance of sexuality and romance in tandem. It is informative to note that the word *sex* comes from the Latin *secare* ("to section, divide"), suggesting the ancient myth of Hermaphrodite, the peculiar creature with two faces, two sets of limbs, and one large body. Hermaphrodite was resented by the gods, who ended up dividing the creature into two biologically separate sections—male and female, each with its sexual characteristics, including differential seductive faces.

Sexual desire is embedded in the limbic system, or the group of interconnected deep brain structures which are common to all mammals. This system is involved in emotion, motivation, and various autonomic functions. But evolution has also provided the human brain with the neocortex, which is the source of language, conscious thought, and other rational faculties. This unique kind of brain structure begs a fundamental question with regard to the love-sex opposition: Has the neocortex transformed the *sex* instinct into a conscious act that we have come to call *love*? If so, then it might explain why there is a constant tug of war in us between sexual and romantic feelings, corresponding to the dichotomy between the limbic and neocortical systems. Our myths, legends, and artistic artifacts have essentially dealt with this opposition in powerful ways. The Greeks named it as a difference between *eros* and *agape*. Eros was the god of carnal love. In Greek art he was depicted as a winged youth, often with his eyes covered to symbolize the blindness of love. In the Eros legend, sex is the source of new life and of creativity. Here's how Sigmund Freud put it[17]:

Civilization is a process in the service of Eros, whose purpose is to combine single human individuals, and after that families, then races, peoples and nations, into one great unity, the unity of mankind. Why this has to happen, we do not know; the work of Eros is precisely this.

Agape, on the other hand, represented spiritual (romantic) love as distinct from erotic love. Aphrodite was the mythical personification of agape. Artists and poets have traditionally portrayed Aphrodite as the goddess of love and beauty, even though her functions in ancient Greece were more varied and complex. Many myths suggest that she instigated human love affairs, constituting a counterpart to Cupid. The Da Vinci and Waterhouse paintings above portray *eros* and *agape* iconically and in tandem on the faces of the subjects, thus blending the two seamlessly. It is relevant to note that the tradition of the wedding kiss comes from the early Christian belief in *agape* as a divine binding force, allowing the partners to exchange their souls through their breaths. That act was meant to fulfill the scripture that "the two shall become one flesh" guaranteeing both the amalgamation of *agape* and *eros* and thus of the permanency of the marriage.

The Love Machine

"I'm just a love machine, and I won't work for nobody but you." These are the first lines of a popular 1975 ballad, "Love Machine," by the Miracles, which was recorded again in 1983 by the rock group Wham, becoming one of the most popular songs of the 1980s. *Love machine* is a useful metaphor for the body-in-love—a figurative concept that can be traced back to the 1747 book, *L'homme machine*, by French physician Jacques de la Mettrie, in which he argued that the human body works like a machine.[18] The Miracles' song figuratively conveys the sense that a body-in-love will "work" only if set in motion by a paramour, both romantically and sexually. The metaphor suggests, by extension, that studying the body's "parts"—its gestures, postures, and other witting and unwitting anatomical movements—can provide insights into the "body language" of love. The relevance of this and other metaphors of love will be discussed in the next chapter. Suffice it to say here that the metaphor provides a convenient frame for discussing bodily actions and activities in romance situations.

The scientific study of body language and its "mechanics," to extend the machine metaphor, is called *kinesics*, a field developed initially by the American anthropologist Ray L. Birdwhistell, who used slow-motion films of conversations to analyze speakers' bodily behaviors as they interacted. He borrowed terms and techniques from linguistics to characterize the various motions that made up meaningful body language. He reported the results of his findings in two classic books, titled *Introduction to Kinesics* and *Kinesics and Context*.[19] Kinesic signs can be inborn (unwitting), learned (witting), or a mixture of the two. Blinking the eyes, clearing the throat, and facial flushing are innate (inborn) signs or, more precisely, signals. These are often involuntary. Laughing, crying, and shrugging the shoulders, on the other hand, are examples of mixed signals. They may originate as innate actions and reactions, but cultural rules shape their timing and use. A wink of the eye, a thumbs up motion, or a military salute, on the other hand, are learned (witting) signs. For this reason, their meanings vary culturally.

Body language is perceived as critical by both partners during early romance and courtship. Cocking or tilting the head, assuming an exaggerated tone of voice, displaying a pseudo-nonchalant attitude, raising a shoulder, arching the back, and playing with the hair are part of a performance script conveying romantic interest. The script may vary across cultures, but its courtship or romantic significance does not. For this reason, the love machine's movements may look comical or absurd to outsiders, especially those who are not in love. But to romantic partners they constitute a crucial mode of affective communication at key stages in the enactment of love. So, while human sexual-romantic behaviors may be residues of some ancient animal mate-assessment tendency, as discussed in the previous chapter, the diversity that is evident in them across cultures suggests that they are shaped by history, not only by nature.

Kinesic codes also mediate peoples' perceptions of which bodily parts or zones are erogenous or sexually significant. They possess what semioticians call indexicality; that is to say, the specific body parts are interpreted as signs that index (indicate) some cultural tradition or value pertaining to sexuality and gender. The philosopher-semiotician Michel Foucault argued persuasively that "sins of the flesh" are hardly universal.[20] They can only be understood in some cultural and historical context. The Puritans of England, for instance, saw any form of sexual contact or seductive gazing in a marriage as a kind of "necessary sin"; needless to say, these were strictly prohibited outside of marriage. On the other hand, the many hedonistic rites and practices of contemporary cultures exalt and glorify the eroticism of the human body. Obviously, what is obscene behavior to some is acceptable behavior to others. Nature does not determine which bodily parts and actions are enticing and romantic; humans do. In her fascinating book, *The Gift of Touch*, Helen Colton illustrates how cultures define the sexual parts of the love machine with an ingenious analogy.[21] If a stranger were to come upon a woman taking a bath, then, Colton argues, culture conditions what bodily part or area she would instinctively cover: a Laotian woman might cover her breasts; a Chinese woman might hide her feet; a Sumatran woman would conceal her knees; a Samoan woman would cover her navel; a western woman would cover her breasts with one arm and her genital area with the other hand. Clearly, as Colton's hypothetical scenario suggests, the specific bodily parts that are perceived to be sexual and exposable differ widely from culture to culture. Colton's analogy also brings out the importance of touch in the perceptions of sexuality. More broadly, tactility is a semiotic code that governs the patterns of touch. Holding hands, for example, is a universal sign of affection among friends and family members. But it is especially meaningful in romance as the number of popular love ballads confirm—"The Touch of Your Hand" (Leo Reisman, 1934), "Hold Hands" (Fats Domino, 1961), "I Wanna Hold Your Hand" (The Beatles, 1964), "Hold My Hand" (The Kinks, 1969), among others.

The origin of hand-holding as a sign of intimacy is unknown. The evolutionary importance of the hand can be seen in its prehistoric representations in rock art around the world, acknowledging one of the earliest of the major hominid characteristics to have evolved, distinguishing the human species from its nearest primate relatives—namely, bipedalism or an adaptation to a completely erect posture and a two-footed striding walk. All other mammals utilize four limbs for locomotion. Primates that stand on two have quite different postures and gaits from humans. In evolutionary terms, bipedalism freed the human hand, allowing it to become a supremely sensitive limb for precise manipulation and grasping, in addition to communicating feelings to others via gesticulation and touch. So, it is not out of the question to suggest that the hand-holding gesture emerges at the dawn of human consciousness, indicating that love itself may have been, by inference, one of the first emotional states experienced as significant by our species. The importance of hand-holding in love situations may also explain the reason why rings have been exchanged for romantic reasons since antiquity. In Italian, the wedding ring is called *fede* (faithfulness), which is an abbreviation of *mani in fede* (hands clasped in faith), which suggests, in turn, that rings are material symbols standing for the act of faith. Tactile romantic communication is not limited, of course, to hand-holding. Linking arms, putting one's arm around the shoulder to indicate intimacy, hugging to convey happiness, are common interrelated signs. Anthropologists are unclear as to why such tactile behavior varies across cultures. This may be related to the fact that body parts are interpreted differentially as indexical signs throughout the world, as already mentioned.[22] Hand-holding, however, appears to be a universal sign of affection.

Another metaphorical aspect of the love machine involves hugging, which is an action that breaks the interpersonal "zone barrier," called more technically a *proxemic* space, a phenomenon first examined systematically by the American anthropologist Edward T. Hall in the late 1950s.[23] As a soldier during World War II, Hall had noticed that people maintained recognizable zones among themselves during conversations, coming soon to realize that many (if not most) breakdowns in communication were attributable to infractions of these zone barriers. The unconscious differences in the ways that people of diverse cultures perceive interpersonal zones and the ways they behave within them play a powerful role in influencing the outcomes of face-to-face interactions. Hall measured and assessed these critical interpersonal zones with statistical techniques, finding that they varied according to age, gender, and other social variables.

Some proxemic patterns seem to be universal. For example, the immediate physical zone around a human being constitutes a sphere of privacy and intimacy. The size of the zone will vary somewhat from culture to culture, but all people perceive this close zone as an intimate one. Hugging fits into this zone, which, Hall surmises, is rooted in our biological past, and is thus based on our innate sense of the significance of emotional proximity. In this zone, the senses are activated and the presence of the other is unmistakable. This phase is reserved for lovers, conveying a sense of intimacy, as well as for friends and family members, for communicating comfort and protection. The actual dimensions may vary somewhat, but the hugging zone has a universal meaning based on affection and love.

The proxemic zone of intimacy is also where dancing fits in as a means to convey romantic feelings through rhythmically suggestive bodily movements. Dance serves various functions in human life, not just courtship. It can be a form of aesthetic communication, expressing emotions, moods, ideas, etc. It also has ritualistic-sacred functions, as for example, in some Sub-Saharan African societies which engage in masked dances to exorcise spirits. All societies have characteristic forms of dance, which take place at ceremonial occasions or at gatherings. By dancing together, members express their sense of common identity or belonging. The best known form of aesthetic dancing is *ballet*, which originated in the courts of Italy and France during the Renaissance, becoming a professional artistic discipline shortly thereafter. It is relevant to note that virtually every major ballet revolves around romance and its fulfillment or failure. Tchaikovsky's, *Swan Lake* (1875–1876), *Sleeping Beauty* (1890), Prokofiev's *Romeo and Juliet* (1935), Adam's *Giselle* (1861), among many others, deal with the power and tragedy of love. Early precursors to ballets were the lavish court dances of Renaissance Italy, which translated the courtly love poetry into dance, thus indicating a direct link between the body-in-love and the mind-in-love. Professional ballet dancers first appeared in the mid-1600s, with the art form being developed extensively during the reign of Louis XIV of France.

The great ballets mentioned above revolve around *agape*. Needless to say, *eros* surfaces as well in the dance form. One of the most erotically suggestive of all dances is the Argentinian tango, which gained worldwide popularity during the 1910s, initiating a craze for Latin ballroom dancing in Paris, London, and New York City. Its inherent sexuality became a cultural obsession after matinée idol Rudolph Valentino and his partner featured the tango in the motion picture *Four Horsemen of the Apocalypse* (1921). Its sensual-erotic power was revived by *Scent of a Woman* (1992), which features a passionate tango danced by Robert De Niro and a young lady, Gabrielle Anwar, who is literally swept off her feet by the erotic sway of the tango "Por una cabeza." The dance conveys passion through alternate long and slow steps as well as short and quick ones, with sudden turns and suggestive poses. Pacino is blind, but as the scene suggests, the tango engages more primal bodily senses that do not require sight. Courtship practices have traditionally attempted to curtail such seductive impulses, utilizing forms of "safe dancing" controlled by elders overlooking the event. But the tango's power over us cannot be denied, and we continue to indulge it to this day.

Body language, to reiterate, is especially significant during courtship periods and tends to be gendered. However, models of gender in modern societies are flexible and constantly changing. Our view of masculinity, for example, has changed drastically in only a few decades. The Fonz on *Happy Days*—a paean to 1950s aloof masculinity in matters of romance—has morphed into the Leonard of *The Big Bang Theory* who demonstrates a more sentimental affective attachment to his paramour (and then wife), Penny. If the TV sitcoms are correct, then "macho man" is morphing more and more into a "geek man." Nonetheless, surveys continue to show that men still think that emotional aloofness is part of how they should behave in courtship; that is, they continue to see romantic involvement as too feminine and undesirable, as is evident in another television program, *Mad Men*, although the program portrays the macho man in an ambivalent way, as hiding his emotional feelings detrimentally.[24] Simply put, today's men are searching for a way to reconcile old ideas with new models of masculinity. In the comedic movie *Knocked Up* (2007), a slacker, played by Seth Rogen, would hardly be perceived as a role model for a perfect partner—he is lazy, unkempt, rude, and a pot smoker. He has none of the qualities that we have traditionally assigned to the ideal mate—good looks, money, social status, charm, etc. He is neither a macho man nor a geek. Yet somehow Rogan becomes entangled romantically with an intelligent, beautiful, and successful television journalist, played by Katherine Heigl. Is this an absurd fantasy of slacker scriptwriters? The enormous success of the film would argue against this, because it also appealed broadly to young women. The lure of the tall and good-looking paramour, endowed with a "noble mien," which comes from the traditions associated with the chivalric code, may have weakened considerably today.

Clothing and the Body in Love

Originally, clothes were designed to enhance survivability by providing protection against the elements; they were, in other words, fabricated as prosthetic additions to bodily hair and skin thickness. As Werner Enninger aptly points out, this is why clothing styles have varied according to geography and topography: "The distribution of types of clothing in relation to different climatic zones and the variation in clothes worn with changes in weather conditions show their practical, protective function."[25] But as social life expanded in the early communities and groups, clothes were transformed semiotically into *dress codes* (from Old French *dresser* "to arrange, set up") that informed people how to dress themselves in social situations, including in romantic ones, beyond any protective function. In the 1830s, Darwin traveled to the islands of Tierra del Fuego, off the southern tip of South America, where he saw people wearing only a little paint and a small cloak made of animal skin, in spite of the cold rain and the sleet.[26] Darwin gave the people scarlet cloth, which they took and wrapped around their necks. It was evident to Darwin that even in the cold weather, these people wore clothing more for social reasons than for protection.

Clothing is connected to fertility rites and to concepts of sexuality and modesty. As the anthropologist Helen Fisher observes, even in the jungle of Amazonia, where clothing serves virtually no protective function against the elements, Yanomamo men and women wear clothes for sexual modesty.[27] A Yanomamo woman would feel as much discomfort at removing her genital string belt as would a North American woman if she were to remove her clothes in public. Similarly, a Yanomamo man would feel just as much embarrassment at his genitals accidentally falling out of their encasement as would a North American male caught literally "with his pants down." Clothing has, in fact, always played a role in matters of morality and in courtship displays and practices. When a young Zulu woman falls in love, she is expected traditionally to make a beaded necklace resembling a close-fitting collar with a flat panel attached, which she then gives to her prospective mate. The necklace is a courtship gift designed to convey a specific type of romantic message: for example, a combination of pink and white beads in a certain pattern would convey the message "You are poor, but I love you just the same."[28]

No one knows exactly when people first wore clothes for social reasons. They probably began to make and wear them more than 100,000 years ago. The archeological record shows that a prehistoric hunter may have worn the skin of a bear or a reindeer not only to keep warm but also as a sign of personal skill, bravery, and strength as a hunter. By the end of the Old Stone Age—about 25,000 years ago—people had invented the needle, which enabled them to sew skins together. They had also learned to make yarn from the threadlike parts of some plants and from the fur or hair of some animals. In addition, they had learned to weave yarn into cloth. At the same time, people had begun to raise plants that gave them a steady supply of materials for making yarn. They had also started to herd sheep and other animals that gave them wool.

Women and men in the ancient civilizations developed clothing styles to mark their social status and to emphasize their attractiveness. In ancient Egypt, for example, men wore loincloths and long garments with a sash at the waist, so as to emphasize the muscular features of the male body. Women wore full-length wraparound gowns and close-fitting sheaths, which enhanced the female figure. Dress codes with similar functions can be found across the ancient world. After Charlemagne became Holy Roman Emperor in 800 CE, a relatively uniform dress code appeared in Europe. Charlemagne's own every-day attire consisted of an undertunic and an overtunic, with breeches cross-gartered to the knee. This introduced the "tunic style" to other European monarchs, setting them apart from peasants. Court ladies also started wearing long tunics, under supertunics hitched up to show the tunics beneath. A cloth veil concealed the hair. These garments made up the basic wardrobe of the European aristocracy up until the Middle Ages. It was intended to convey modesty and restraint. In the 1100s, luxurious Oriental fabrics and styles were brought to Europe, leading to a dress code that became symbolic of the new courtly love culture. The trailing tunic and tight pants became the main form of dress for young men in the 1300s, designed to enhance their masculine features. In the same era, young women started wearing tightly-fitting corsets to shape the female figure.

In the Renaissance, the development of new fabrics and materials brought about a desire for elaborate styles. By the early 1600s, fashion sensibility spread throughout the social classes. The dress code included lace edges, frills at the neck and sleeves, collars that eventually became the cravat and the necktie, and breeches for men. This period also saw the introduction of the wig for men and women. The same era made high heel shoes become part of a new fashionable dress code. High heel shoes are elegant, stylish, and sexy. In fourteenth-century Venice noble women wore them to set themselves apart socially from peasant women. The sixteenth century monarch, Caterina de' Medici, wore high heel shoes for her marriage to Henry II in Paris in 1533. The event kindled a fad among the aristocracy (male and female), encouraged by Louis XIV of France, who apparently wore them to increase his modest height. It was in the mid-nineteenth century that heeled shoes—low-cut, laced or buttoned to the ankle—became a fashion craze among all women, who wore them to keep up their dresses from dragging along the ground and to emphasize their figure. The reason for this is obvious—high heels force the body to tilt, raising the buttocks and giving prominence to the breasts. They also give glimpses of the woman's feet in a tantalizing manner, thus accentuating the role of feet as fetishes in the history of sexuality, as William Rossi has illustrated.[29]

Fashions considered appropriate for men and women have changed as standards and conceptualizations of masculinity and femininity have changed. Until the late 1700s, upper-class European men dressed as elaborately as women did. It was acceptable for them to wear bright-colored or pastel suits trimmed with gold and lace, hats decorated with feathers, high-heeled shoes, and fancy jewelry. With the French Revolution came radical changes, as men began wearing trousers for the first time in six hundred years. No radical changes in men's clothing has taken place since. Women's fashion reverted to what was deemed the "classical style," a look featuring thin fabrics and bare arms—emphasizing a new sense of freedom from the yoke of puritanical strictures. The Industrial Revolution of the nineteenth century projected fashion for the masses into the realm of economic possibility. Since then fashion for everyone has become an intrinsic feature of modern living. By midnineteenth century, men abandoned any style based on flamboyance in favor of plain, dark-colored wool suits. Society came to view this style as part of the emerging business dress code. Until the early 1900s, European and American women rarely wore trousers, and their skirts almost always covered their ankles. By the 1920s, however, standards of feminine modesty had changed to the point that women began to wear both trousers and shorter skirts. As semiotician Roland Barthes pointed out, fashion changes constantly because rapid turnover guarantees economic success. It is the only constant in fashion.[30]

Needless to say, clothing and fashion have also played important roles in the theater and more recently in popular culture (in movies, television, fashion shows, etc.). The use of costumes to represent themes, characters, etc. through theatrical performance started with the Greeks, although costumes in rituals are found across the world and across time. The Italian Commedia dell'Arte used costumes to bring out the archetypal features of the characters. It started in the late Middle Ages in Italy, with stock comedic characters such as the acrobat Arlecchino (Harlequin), who wore a cat-like mask and motley colored clothes, and who carried a bat or wooden sword, the predecessor of the vaudevillian slapstick. His crony, Brighella, was more roguish and sophisticated, a cowardly villain who would do anything for money. Pagliaccio (the clown) was the forerunner of today's clownish stand-up comedian. Pulcinella (Punch), a dwarfish humpback with a crooked nose, and a cruel bachelor who chased young girls, also has many descendants today in television and movie comedians. Pantalone (Pantaloon) was a caricature of the Venetian merchant, rich and retired, mean and miserly, with a young wife and an adventurous daughter. Il Dottore (the doctor), his only friend, was a caricature of the pseudo-intellectual—pompous and fraudulent. In all cases, the costumes reflected character.

The human being is the only animal that does not "go nude," so to speak, without triggering off some form of social repercussion (unless, of course, the social ambiance is that of a nudist camp or some other context that accepts nudity as normal). Nudity can only be interpreted culturally. We are all born nude, but we soon learn that nudity has specific connotations. What is considered "exposable" of the body will vary significantly from culture to culture, even though the covering of genitalia seems, for the most part, to cross cultural boundaries. Michel Foucault has suggested that clothing the body has, paradoxically, stimulated curiosity and desire in the body itself.[31] Covering the body is an act of modesty, but, as Foucault suggests, this has imbued it with a kind of secret desirability below the covered surface. So, at a striptease performance, the shedding of clothes does several symbolic things at once: it removes imposed moral restrictions on sexuality; it reveals those covered bodily parts that have become desirable; it engages viewers in a communal ritual similar to the many carnivals put on throughout the world. The nude body is, in a word, a sign system. This is why visual artists have always had a fascination with the nude figure. The ancient Greek and Roman nude statues of male warriors, Michelangelo's powerful *David* sculpture, Rodin's nude sculpture *The Thinker* are all suggestive of the potency of the male body. It is this kind of body image that is an unconscious archetype that influences our views of the attractiveness of the male in our society. A male with a skinny body is hardly ever perceived as sexually attractive, at least according to our representational practices. On the other side of this semiotic paradigm, paintings and sculptures of female nude figures have tended to portray the body ambiguously as soft in outline, yet still sensuous, as can be seen in the famous ancient statue known as the Venus (Aphrodite) de Milo, sculpted by Alexandros of Antioch around 150 BCE (Fig. 2.4):

Fig. 2.4 *Aphrodite de Milo (Alexandros, c. 150 BCE)* (Wikimedia Commons)

The ancient paintings and sculptures reveal the artist's interpretation of the "ideal" attractive body. Perhaps no one like Da Vinci brought out the inherent beauty of idealized human proportions in his art, as can be seen in his classic drawing of *Vitruvian Man* (Fig. 2.5):

Encircled by two perfect geometric figures, the circle and the square, with the various proportions in the limbs drawn according to the golden ratio, Da Vinci's painting is a marvelous interpretation of this ratio, which intrigued philosophers, artists, and mathematicians in antiquity, and which Renaissance painters called the *divine proportion*. It is widely accepted that a figure or form incorporating this ratio exhibits a special beauty.

On the other representational side, throughout history we have also made fun of the body, starting with ancient graffiti in public squares, which are essentially caricatures of the body and its disproportions. The art of caricature was common among the ancient Egyptians and Greeks. It was revived by Italian Renaissance artists and developed throughout Europe in the eighteenth century to ridicule political, social, or religious people, groups, or institutions. Comedic theater and narratives emerged as well to mock love relations and the obsession with attractiveness through clothing and other accouterments of fashion. Mockery of the body and fashion was a subtext in the mid-1970s

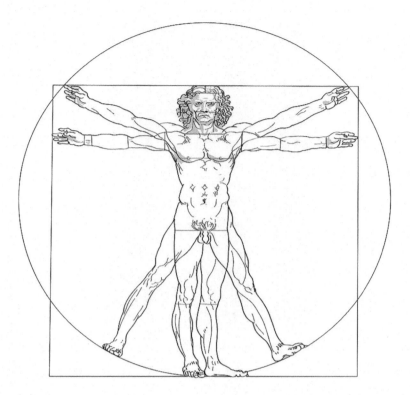

Fig. 2.5 *Vitruvian Man (Leonardo Da Vinci, c. 1490)* (Wikimedia Commons)

Rocky Horror Picture Show, which was intentionally transgressive of gender categories and their attendant dress codes. As Greenwald has observed, the show favored "cross dressing, and an overall smearing of the lines between the sexes."[32] The show initiated a cross-gender and transgender movement within pop culture that included musicians such as Kiss, Michael Jackson, Alice Cooper, and Marilyn Manson. The *Rocky Horror Picture Show* debuted in 1975 in Britain. It was carnivalesque sexual theater at its best, mocking traditional gender roles, fashion practices, and pseudo-morality. It has become a tradition in many areas of the world for the event to take place at midnight on Halloween, when patrons show up dressed in drag and lingerie. Like the ancient and medieval carnivals, the audience is not only part of the show; it is the show. Audiences dance and sing, shout lewd comments at the screen, and throw objects at certain points, such as toast, toilet paper, water, or rice. The master of ceremonies, called sardonically Dr. Frank-N-Furter, instructs and exhorts the audience with the following words:

Give yourself over to absolute pleasure. Swim the warm waters of sins of the flesh—erotic nightmares beyond any measure, and sensual daydreams to treasure forever. Can't you just see it? Don't dream it, be it.

To his entreaty audience members indulge themselves in "absolute pleasure" by drinking alcohol and smoking. *Rocky Horror* never made it into mainstream movie theaters because its carnivalesque elements were so transgressive at the time that, as the movie itself warned, in parodic imitation of censorship ratings: "Society must be protected. You're lifestyle is too extreme." The use of the word *Horror* in the spectacle is significant. Horror movies have, arguably, the same psychological function of the freak sideshows of the circus. Like P. T. Barnum's sideshows, the horror genre taps into our fascination with, and fear of, the grotesque. As British film critic Robin Wood aptly observes, "One might say that the true subject of the horror genre is the struggle for recognition of all that our civilization represses and oppresses," including our inability to face our "nothingness and probable purposelessness."[33]

Deconstructing Gender

The discussion of the *Rocky Horror Picture Show* and it deconstruction of gender brings us to the doorsteps of the late French philosophers Jacques Derrida and Michel Foucault, who saw cultural codes such as the gender one as artificial constructions based on shifting worldviews.[34] Their goal was to "deconstruct" these by showing how our traditional assumptions about categories such as sexuality and gender are culturally inward-looking. Thus, what people think is "natural" turns out to be "constructed."

Unlike sex and love, which have a basis in the body and the emotions (Worlds 1 and 2), gender is, as already argued, a construction of culture (World 3). Its deconstruction really started at the turn of the twentieth century with the Dada movement in art. For example, the Dadaist painter Marcel Duchamp, who struggled immensely with his own sexual identity, was among the first to experiment with ambiguous perceptions of masculinity through public adoptions of his female alter ego, Rrose Sélavy, challenging the normalcy of gender codes with his iconic painting, *The Bride Stripped Bare by Her Bachelors, Even* (1915–1923). The painting is an attempt to deconstruct gender relations as meaningless fragments of signs, in true Dadaist fashion, begging the question famously asked by Ursula Le Guin, "Is gender necessary?"[35]

The deconstruction of masculinity was the theme of a fascinating art exhibit at the Musée d'Orsay in Paris from September 2013 to January 2014, with the title, *Masculine/Masculine: The Nude Man in Art from 1800 to the Present Day*, and the following description[36]:

> While it has been quite natural for the female nude to be regularly exhibited, the male nude has not been accorded the same treatment. It is highly significant that until the show at the Leopold Museum in Vienna in the autumn of 2012, no exhibition had opted to take a fresh approach, over a long historical perspective, to the representation of the male nude. However, male nudity was for a long time, from the 17th to 19th centuries, the basis of traditional Academic art training and a key element in Western creative art

One of the posters used to promote the exhibit conveyed the ambiguity in gender terms of the masculine form that starts in mythological antiquity. The figure in the poster is that of a young and muscular male body, but the face could easily be interpreted as that of a female (Fig. 2.6):

Fig. 2.6 *Poster Promoting "Masculine/Masculine" (Musée d'Orsay, 2013)*

The ambiguity is also expressed in the slash used in the title of the exhibit, indicating that there is an inbuilt opposition between male and female characteristics that often become amalgamated in gender perceptions. As is well known, the psychiatrist, Carl Jung called this opposition the *animus-anima* archetypal conflict within us.[37] The *anima* is the feminine sense in all of us; the *animus*, the corresponding masculine sense; and the *persona*, representing the face is the role we present to the world. Michael Sims has observed that modern-day deconstructions of gender are not much different from ancient ones, as can be seen in the famous "Venus Impudique" case. As he puts it: "Typical early representations of…the body include the Venus Impudique, the Shameless Venus discovered in France in 1864. It is a three-inch piece of mammoth ivory, a female figure that apparently was carved, sometime around 14,000 BCE, in its current state: headless, armless, footless, without any specifically modeled features except the vertical slit of the vagina."[38] As a major semiotic technique, deconstruction has receded somewhat, but it left its residues in various domains of aesthetic semiotics. Gender codes are reifications of changing perceptions of the body and its relation to sexuality and romance. They change over time, thus deconstructing themselves—in effect, semiotics is best when it documents, not assails, the spontaneous deconstructions of meaning in specific eras.

Epilogue

The representational history of the body-in-love in myths, literature, and art documents how romantic traditions across the world have unfolded and what they have meant to people at specific eras of time. The body is a primary source of signification, and a vehicle for understanding the connection between nature and culture in human life. The body, the face, the hands and other parts of the body allow us to represent and communicate, wittingly and unwittingly, intentions, roles, impressions, needs, and above all else our emotions. Discoveries in neuroscience have shown that nonverbal signs are produced and processed differently from words. Spoken language is processed in the cerebral cortex, a more developed area of the brain that is unique to human beings. In contrast, nonverbal cues—such as smiling, staring, and clenching the fists—are processed in lower, more primitive areas such as the limbic system. People often produce and receive nonverbal cues without conscious awareness of doing so.

The human body consists of some 25 trillion cells, or about 2000 times the number of living creatures, and these have direct or indirect connections with one another through messages delivered by sign structures. The sheer density of such connections is staggering. Only a minuscule fraction is known to us, let alone understood. Interior messages include information about the significance of one somatic scheme for all of the others, for each over-all control grid (such as the immune system), and for the entire integrative regulatory circuitry. The body-in-love appears to activate all kinds of somatic schemes and circuitry, affecting facial expression, posture, proxemic patterns, and the like in specific ways as we have seen in this chapter. In turn, these affect how we represent and perceive romance, gender, and traditions such as marriage.

The brain is a flexible structure that is constantly adapting to new conditions—or to use current terminology, it is "rewiring" itself all the time. One area in which this is evident is the changing perceptions of the relation between love, courtship, sexuality, and marriage in modernity. In one relevant 2011 study, Anthony Paik found a correlation between the period of sexual debut (early or late adolescence) and subsequent marriage stability.[39] Drawing on a sample of 3793 married couples from the 2002 National Survey of Family Growth, he found that first-marriage dissolutions correlated with the period of sexual debut—the later the debut the more the marriage tended to be stable. Similar studies have shown that premarital sex with partners other than the ones that end up in marriage increases the risks of marital dissolution.[40] A study by Busby, Willoughby, and Carroll, for example, showed that premarital promiscuity had negative effects on marriage stability.[41] The objective was to test whether the number of sexual partners was associated with sexual quality, communication, relationship satisfaction, and stability, while controlling for relationship length, education, race, income, age, and religiosity. With a sample of 2654 married individuals, the study found that the larger number of sexual partners correlated directly with lower levels of sexual quality, communication, and relationship stability, providing support for a "sexual restraint theory." Gender was not significantly associated with the patterns in the model but age cohorts did have different patterns. Lehmiller, Vanderdrift, and Kelly studied friends-with-benefits relationships, based on an Internet sample of individuals currently involved in such relationships.[42] The results indicated that sexual activity was a common motivation for men to begin such relationships, whereas emotional connection was a more common one for women. In addition, men were more likely to hope that the relationship remained the same over time, whereas women expressed more desire for change into either a full-fledged romance or a basic friendship. Unexpectedly, both men and women were more committed to the friendship than to the sexual aspect of the relationship.

When viewed cumulatively, the research is documenting a reconstruction process (as opposed to deconstruction) of the sex-love-culture (body-mind-environment) continuum, affecting traditional courtship practices. In most dating scenarios of the past, there would be parental supervision or chaperoning of some kind. By the early twentieth century, this changed, as open sexuality became condoned more and more. It is humorous to look back at instructional film shorts about dating for teenagers, which were made by adult educators in the 1950s who were afraid of a growing open sexuality in society. Those films replaced the chaperones, and were mainly cautionary tales of all the bad things that would happen if teens engaged in sex on a date. Today, by and large, there are no chaperones, cautionary tale videos, or parental supervision; there are health courses taught in schools and websites that offer patchy disconnected advice. In this modern scenario, love seems to be either taken for granted or marginalized as too idealistic, with sexuality and gender identity taking center stage. In effect, the emphasis has shifted to *eros*, away from *agape*. But the history of romance shows this to be misguided, because in the end the human condition is based on seeking ideals. The fulfillment of romantic love is one of those and, as far as can be told, is still directive of human aspirations.

Notes

1. The relevant research can be found in Sheril Kirshenbaum, *The Science of Kissing: What Our Lips Are Telling Us* (New York: Grand Central, 2011).
2. Desmond Morris, Peter Collett, Peter Marsh, and Marie O'Shaughnessy, *Gestures: Their Origins and Distributions* (London: Cape, 1979).
3. See Michel Foucault, *The History of Sexuality* (London: Allen Lane, 1976).
4. See, for example, Paul Ekman, *Darwin and Facial Expression: A Century of Research in Review* (New York: Academic, 1973); "Movements with Precise Meanings," *Journal of Communication* 26 (1976): 14–26; "The Classes of Nonverbal Behavior," in W. Raffler-Engel (ed.), *Aspects of Nonverbal Communication*, pp. 89–102 (Lisse: Swets and Zeitlinger, 1980); "Methods for Measuring Facial Action," in K. R. Scherer and P. Ekman (eds.), *Handbook of Methods in Nonverbal Behavior*, pp. 45–90 (Cambridge: Cambridge University Press, 1982); *Telling Lies* (New York: Norton, 1985); and *Emotions Revealed* (New York: Holt, 2003).
5. Charles Darwin, *The Expression of the Emotions in Man and Animals* (London: John Murray, 1872).
6. Margaret Mead, *Continuities in Cultural Evolution* (New Haven: Yale University Press, 1964).

7. See Silvan Tomkins and Carroll E. Izard, *Affect, Cognition, and Personality: Empirical Studies* (New York: Springer, 1965).

8. See, for example, Marcel Danesi, *The Semiotics of Emoji* (London: Bloomsbury, 2016).

9. Stephen R. Peck, *Atlas of Facial Expression* (Oxford: Oxford University Press, 1987); Mark Simon, *Facial Expression* (New York: Watson-Guptill, 2005).

10. Desmond Morris, *The Human Zoo* (London: Cape, 1969); Desmond Morris, Peter Collett, Peter Marsh, and Marie O'Shaughnessy, *Gestures: Their Origins and Distributions* (London: Cape, 1979).

11. Starkey Duncan and Donald W. Fiske, *Face-to-Face Interaction* (Hillsdale, NJ: Erlbaum, 1977); Jan Latiolais-Hargrave, *Strictly Business: Body Language: Using Nonverbal Communication for Power and Success* (Iowa: Kent Hunt Publishing, 2008).

12. Angus Trumble, *A Brief History of the Smile* (New York: Basic, 2004), pp. 49–50.

13. Dennis Lin, Jilin Tu, Shyamsundar Rajaram, Zhenqui Zhang, and Thomas Huang, "Da Vinci's Mona Lisa: A Modern Look at a Timeless Classic," in S. Renals, S. Bengio, and J. G. Fiscus (eds.), *Machine Learning for Multimodal Interaction* MLMI 2006, *Lecture Notes in Computer Science*, volume 4299 (Berlin: Springer, 2006).

14. Debbie Nathan, *Pornography* (Toronto: Groundwork Books, 2007).

15. Herodotus, *The Histories*, Library of Alexandria 2014, originally 440 BCE.

16. James Frazer, *The Golden Bough* (London: Macmillan, 1890).

17. Sigmund Freud, *Civilization and its Discontents* (London: Hogarth, 1963, originally 1931), p. 48.

18. See Aram Vartanian, *La Mettrie's "L'homme machine:" A Study in the Origins of an Idea* (Princeton: Princeton University Press, 1960).

19. Ray L. Birdwhistell, *Introduction to Kinesics* (Ann Arbor: University of Ann Arbor, 1952); *Kinesics and Context: Essays on Body Motion Communication* (Harmondsworth: Penguin, 1970).

20. Foucault, *The History of Sexuality*, op. cit.

21. Helen Colton, *Telling Lies* (New York: Norton, 1983).

22. Edward T. Hall, *The Hidden Dimension* (New York: Doubleday, 1966).

23. Edward T. Hall, *The Silent Language* (Greenwich: Fawcett, 1959); *Beyond Culture* (Garden City: Anchor, 1976).

24. Nicky Falkoff, "The Father, the Failure and the Self-Made Man: Masculinity in *Mad Men*," *Critical Quarterly* 54 (2012): 31–45.

25. Werner Enninger, "Clothing," in R. Bauman (ed.), *Folklore, Cultural Performances, and Popular Entertainments*, p. 215 (Oxford: Oxford University Press, 1992).

26. Charles Darwin, *The Voyage of the Beagle* (Harmondsworth: Penguin, 1989, originally 1839).

27. Helen Fisher, *Anatomy of Love* (New York: Norton, 1992), pp. 253–254.

28. Lois Sherr Dubin, *The History of Beads* (New York: Abrams, 1987), p. 134.

29. William Rossi, *The Sex Lives of the Foot and Shoe* (New York: Dutton, 1976).

30. Roland Barthes, *Système de la mode* (Paris: Seuil, 1967).

31. Foucault, *The History of Sexuality*, op. cit.

32. Ted Greenwald, *Rock & Roll* (New York: Friedman, 1992), p. 53.

33. Robin Wood, *Hollywood from Vietnam to Reagan* (New York: Columbia University Press, 1979), p. 23.

34. See Jacques Derrida, *Of Grammatology*, trans. by G. C. Spivak (Baltimore: Johns Hopkins Press, 1976); Michel Foucault, *The Archeology of Knowledge*, trans. by A. M. Sheridan Smith (New York: Pantheon, 1972).

35. Ursula K. Le Guin, "Is Gender Necessary?" in *Aurora: Beyond Equality*, edited by Susan Anderson and Vonda McIntyre (Greenwich: Fawcett, 1976), p. 24.

36. http://www.musee-orsay.fr/index.php?id=649&L=1&tx_ttnews[tt_news].

37. See Carl G. Jung, *The Essential Jung* (Princeton: Princeton University Press, 1983).

38. Michael Sims, *Adam's Navel: A Natural and Cultural History of the Human Form* (Harmondsworth: Penguin, 2003).

39. Anthony Paik, "Adolescent Sexuality and the Risk of Marital Dissolution," *Journal of Marriage and Family* 73 (2011): 472–485.

40. See, for example, Jay Teachman, "Premarital Sex, Premarital Cohabitation, and the Risk of Subsequent Marital Dissolution Among Women," *Journal of Marriage and Family* 65 (2003): 444–455.

41. Dean M. Busby, Brian J. Willoughby, and Jason S. Carroll, "Sowing Wild Oats: Valuable Experience or a Field Full of Weeds?" *Personal Relationships* 20 (2013): 706–713.

42. Justin J. Lehmiller, Laura E. Vanderdrift, and Janice R. Kelly, "Sex Differences in Approaching Friends with Benefits Relationships," *Journal of Sex Research* 48 (2011): 275–284.

3

The Language of Love

When love is not madness, it is not love.
—Pedro Calderón de la Barca (1600–1681)

Prologue

If a child were to asks us "What is love?" we would know that it is pointless to give the child a dictionary-type answer such as "an affective response to amorous signals or states." Instead, we would intuitively resort to one of the most fundamental of all discourse strategies—we would connect the concept of love to the child's involvement in situations or experiences that the child can recognize emotionally: "Well, you know, love is the feeling you get when your mommy or daddy kisses and hugs you." We might also read the child a story that illustrates what love is all about, such as a fable or fairy tale that revolves around this emotion.

The analogies and stories we tell children are products of unconscious metaphorical reasoning, which allows us to make abstractions understandable in concrete ways. Metaphor is more than a fact of language; it is a faculty of mind that reveals how we connect things into abstractions. By and large people might think of it as a stylistic or rhetorical device, used by poets and orators to make their messages more effective or ornate. If the research on metaphor is even partially correct, then it is hardly such a device, even though it is indeed used expertly by poets. Metaphorical reasoning is part of a connective sign

© The Author(s) 2019
M. Danesi, *The Semiotics of Love*, Semiotics and Popular Culture,
https://doi.org/10.1007/978-3-030-18111-6_3

system that reveals how abstract thinking unfolds unconsciously. This is why we used it to allow our hypothetical child to grasp the concept *love* in a concrete way. George Lakoff and Mark Johnson, modern-day pioneers in the study of metaphor, have put it aptly as follows[1]:

> Metaphor is for most people a device of the poetic imagination and the rhetorical flourish—a matter of extraordinary rather than ordinary language. Moreover, metaphor is typically viewed as characteristic of language alone, a matter of words rather than thought and action…We have found, on the contrary, that metaphor is pervasive in everyday life, not just in language but in thought and action.

So, another semiotic way to gain access to the meaning of love in human life is to examine the language used to describe, explain, or characterize it, and how it informs romantic practices and traditions, including poetic ones that go back considerably in time. Recall the *love machine* metaphor discussed in the previous chapter. As the Miracles' song suggested, portraying the body-in-love as a *machine* is something that we can grasp concretely, since the actions and activities of a person in love seem to unfold in an imaginary sense like those of machinery. We can see (in our minds) how physical machines actually "work"; but we can only imagine how love "works"—hence the metaphor. The ontological linkage between love and machines is the reason why we commonly use mechanical terms in conversations about love: "Our love is *working*"; "Their romance is *breaking down*"; "Theirs is a *smoothly running* relationship"; "Their love is starting to *sputter*"; and so on and so forth. The *love machine* metaphor is one of many that permeate our language of love, allowing us to dissect it into its functions, complexities, and vicissitudes within the imagination.

Metaphor is revelatory of the unconscious cultural impressions and experiences that people across the world deem as essential and meaningful. English-speaking societies use words such as *sweet, attractive, passionate, fiery, enchanting*, and the like to portray the effects of love. Each one is a metaphorical capsule that exposes specific cultural perceptions and practices that are intrinsically intertwined. For instance, the *love-is-a-sweet-taste* metaphor not only underlies linguistic expressions such as "She's my *sweetheart*," "I love my *honey*," etc.; it is also connected historically with symbols and rituals, such as the giving of sweets to a loved one on Valentine's Day, eating cake at weddings, going on a "honeymoon"; and so on. These are not isolated happenstance practices—they are interconnected semiotically through metaphorical reasoning.

Words of Love

In his research on the aboriginal tongues of North America in the 1920s and 1930s, Columbia University linguist Franz Boas came to the conclusion that languages served people as classificatory devices for coming to grips with their particular environmental and social realities.[2] For example, he noted that Inuit languages had several terms for the animal we call a *seal*: one is the general term for the animal; another renders the idea of "seal basking in the sun;" and a third of "seal floating on a piece of ice." The Inuit have developed a specialized vocabulary because of the important role played by seals in their communal life. This does not imply, however, that people of different languages cannot understand the Inuit's vocabulary constructions. The paraphrases used above to convey the meanings of their terms show that there are always ways that the resources of any language can be used to understand the concepts of another language. Clearly, language tells an unconscious story of how we think and how we select and etch into words what is important to us.

As far as can be determined, every language has coined words for labeling the concept of love. In English, the word *love* comes from an Indo-European root that means "desire." The same root is also the source of our words *libido* and *lust*, indicating that, since the beginning, *love* and *lust* were conceptualized as two sides of the same emotion. The meaning of *love* as separate from *lust* is a later semantic split, emerging at the time of the chivalric code, as Old English texts corroborate. Words for love in ancient languages showed a similar understanding of the ambiguous nature of love. The Greeks had six terms for love, as mentioned, with *agape* and *eros* forming an opposition differentiating spiritual love from sexual desire. The propensity to name the various feelings and desires associated with love and romance is universal. In Mandarin Chinese, for example, the standard word for love is *Ai*, and the character is, 愛, which has a heart in the middle, indicating that love was located in the heart rather than in the sexual organs—a distinctive metaphor that exists across many languages, including English. When love does not "work out," to return to the *love machine* metaphor, then the correlative metaphor of *heartbreak* occurs in the languages that relate love to the "workings" of the heart.

While single words for *love* and *lust (sex)* seem to have a one-to-one translation correspondence across languages, there are many others that relate to romantic nuances that show cultural differentiation. In Portuguese, *saudade* expresses the sorrow of losing a loved one; in Japanese, *nanpa* indicates the type of flirtatious gaze that is exchanged between two people who are otherwise ashamed to introduce themselves; in Filipino, the word *gigil* designates an urge to connect with someone who is irresistible; in Norwegian, *forelsket* is intended to capture the euphoric feeling produced by romantic love; in Inuit, *iktsuarpok* refers to the feeling of anticipation as one waits for the loved one to arrive; and in Russian, *razbliuto* designates the feeling experienced towards someone who once was, but no longer is, a romantic partner. These are missing as lexical categories in English, even though paraphrases render the relevant ideas in an indirect way. However, since English speakers do not have these available as single word units, they are not inclined to attend to them as being necessary in the understanding of love. The concepts that find expression in the lexicon of a language and in the structure of its phrases and sentences reflect historically-based experiences that are meaningful to those living in a specific culture, as Boas bountifully documented. But the lexicon is not a fixed or finite entity. Speakers of any language can, and do, invent new words and phrases any time they want, according to need or even whim. If for some reason English speakers decided that they needed to refer to the meaning captured by the Inuit term *iktsuarpok* on a consistent basis, then by coining an appropriate word, they would in effect encode this concept into English culture. When a situation with the stated characteristic designated by the new word occurred, English speakers would immediately recognize it, thinking of it as pertaining to a necessary aspect of romance. When we name something, we are imprinting it into our minds indelibly.

All languages have the lexical resources for expressing degrees of love, comparable to English words such as *adore, worship, fancy (someone), have the hots for* (slang), etc. So too do they have antonyms or contrary terms equivalent to English *hate*, the opposite of love, as well as words equivalent to *indifference* or *apathy*, indicating a lack of love, but not its opposite. Terms for sexual activity, on the other hand, are either expressed graphically, with words such as *copulate*, or else with metaphors that describe various aspects of sexuality, most of which are considered taboo or obscene words—the so-called "four-letter" words. Describing sex as *hot, horny, lascivious*, etc. falls under the rubric of metaphorical discourse, constituting a strategy for getting around taboo. It is also relevant to note that *love* and *sex* entail different lexical descriptions. So, if partners are *in love*, then it is more accurate to say that they are on *intimate* terms, rather than engaged in sexual activities. Vice versa, if people are *having sex* for the sake of it, without aspirations to love, then it would be anomalous to say that they are *intimate*. Studies have shown that how we speak about love and sex reveals how we conceptualize this opposition. Harrison and Shortall, for instance, looked at how people in love communicated it to each other.[3]

Responses from 172 college students indicated that the men reported falling in love earlier and expressed it sooner than the women. This might be consistent with the tradition that assigns a pragmatic and cautious view of love to women. Whether or not this is the case, the study showed that we are sensitive to how we speak about love, differentiating it from sex conceptually.

Poets and writers have always been sensitive to the linguistic nuances that love entails, contributing to the development of a "language of love" built on metaphor. Without such a language, there would be no way to reflect consciously on the meanings of love and its counterpart sex. The fact that words for love exist in all languages (as far as can be told) is strong evidence that it is a universal emotion that has meaning to everyone, no matter to what era or culture they belong.

Love Metaphors

A linguistic metaphor is a word, phrase, or expression that is constructed to be representative or symbolic of something by linking it to something else—such as *love* to *sweetness*. From ancient times, metaphor has been seen as one of several rhetorical strategies available to poets and orators to strengthen and embellish their speeches and compositions. But, as it turns out, there is more to metaphor than meets the linguistic eye (metaphorical pun untended). Metaphor reveals how we grasp (not embellish) things through conceptual linkages, as we saw with our explanations of love to a child above.

Metaphors of love abound in all languages, linking this emotion to an infinite array of referents and ideas that can easily be recognized in concrete ways. Some of these in English are illustrated below:

> *Love as a physical attraction (love machine)*
> There were *sparks* between us.
> We are *attracted* to each other.
> My life *revolves* around her.
> I am *magnetically drawn* toward her.

> *Love as a healthy or diseased state*
> Our love is *wholesome*.
> Theirs is a *sick* relationship.
> Their marriage is *dead*; it can't be *revived*.
> Their relationship is in *good shape*.

Love as insanity
I'm *crazy* about her.
He's constantly *raving* about her.
She's *gone mad* over him.
I've *lost my head* over her.

Love as magic
She *cast a spell* over me.
The *magic* in our love is still there after so many years.
She has *bewitched* me.
I'm in a *trance* over her.

Love as gustation
Their love is very *sweet*.
Our relationship has become *sour*.
Their romance has become a *bitter* one.
Our love is still quite *spicy*.

Each metaphor provides a specific perspective on love, allowing us to assign concrete experiential details to this feeling. So, the *physical attraction* metaphor reflects our sense of how two bodies in love seem to work in tandem like the laws of physics, thus connecting love to the properties of matter and energy; the *health-disease* metaphor reveals that we perceive the love-state as affecting a person's mental or physical condition; the *insanity* metaphor mirrors our sense that love is a form of temporary lunacy; the *magic* metaphor betrays our sense that love has the power to influence the course of events as a supernatural force; and the *gustation* metaphor implies that love produces a physical effect on us in the way that gustatory reactions do. As this minimal list shows, metaphor provides us with an array of semantic nuances that can be utilized to project subtle detail onto our understanding of love.

As mentioned briefly above, George Lakoff and Mark Johnson were pioneers in the contemporary study of metaphor.[4] They trace its psychological source to mental images that coalesce from the experience of things. For example, when we say that "Our love is *rising up* within us" or its opposite "Our love is *going down* the drain," we are recruiting our sense of movement from a lower position to a higher one, or vice versa, to grasp the sensation that love (or its lack) produces in us. When we say that "love is *fulfilling*" or that "love has *entered* my soul," we are enlisting our familiarity with the physical nature of entities and substances that can be put into containers or stored in some fashion. The number of such metaphorical domains is limitless. After Lakoff and Johnson, metaphor has come to be perceived among linguists, psychologists, and semioticians as a kind of cognitive template for grasping unconscious abstractions, both internally within language and externally to it, linking various representations, symbols, and practices that exist in a culture. Courtship rituals that reflect a *love-as-a-sweet-taste* metaphor include the use of sweets, such as chocolates, to symbolize romance; the *love-as-magic* metaphor is manifest in the practice of fortune telling and in the use of horoscopes to predict personal romance; the medieval practice of bleeding people to "cure them" of their love is embedded in the *love-as-a-disease* metaphor; the belief that lovers lose their sense of rationality and behave erratically, which reflects *the-love-as insanity* metaphor, is the reason why we explain certain abnormal behaviors, such as Gianciotto's murder of his brother (previous chapter), as "crimes of passion"; and the *love-as-a-physical-attraction* metaphor can easily be seen as inherent in the custom of lovers holding hands or embracing.

Aristotle was the one who coined the term *metaphor*—itself a metaphor (*meta* "beyond" + *pherein* "to carry").[5] The Greek philosopher understood the ability of metaphorical reasoning to shed light on abstract concepts in understandable ways. However, he affirmed that, as conceptually-powerful as it was, the primary function of metaphor was stylistic, a device for sprucing up more prosaic and literal ways of communicating. This latter position became the rule by which metaphor came to be judged until recent times. A pivotal 1977 study by Pollio, Barlow, Fine, and Pollio showed that Aristotle's original view was in effect the correct one.[6] The researchers found that speakers of English uttered, on average, 3000 novel metaphors and 7000 idioms per week. It became clear to linguists and psychologists that metaphor was hardly an optional flourish on literal language. On the contrary, it dominated everyday verbal interactions and was the source of many discourse practices and codes—one of these was romance. Moreover, as subsequent research has extensively documented, metaphorical reasoning interconnects various phases and elements in the history of a culture latently and archetypally, as just mentioned.

Consider a metaphor such as "Love is a rose." The probable source for correlating two apparently unrelated referents seems to be the practice of rose-giving in secret love trysts in the medieval ages, which has linked love to this plant indelibly ever since. In ancient Rome, the rose was a symbol of secrecy. A rose figure was hung over the door to a room where a secret meeting was going on, which was said to be *sub rosa* (under the rose). The rose also symbolized feminine beauty and love in Greek mythology. Chloris, the goddess of flowers, was thought to have created the rose by re-animating the lifeless body of a nymph. The flower was sacred to Aphrodite, constituting her emblem of beauty, and was thought to grow from the blood of Adonis, Aphrodite's paramour. The meaning of the rose as a sign of betrayal started in the medieval courtly love era, when a paramour would leave a rose to a beloved as a secret message to engage in a love affair (as the medieval poetry and stories recount).[7] In his brilliant novel, *The Name of the Rose* (1982), the late semiotician-writer Umberto Eco brings out the subversive aspect of this symbolism perfectly, since it also alluded to the fact that the medieval period was the era in which radical social changes took place under the cloak of secrecy. That was the era as well of the *roman de la rose*, a French allegorical poem introducing the rose into common usage as the symbol of female beauty. It was, arguably, the medievalists who finally gave linguistic and cultural expression to the sense that love itself was an abiding mystery, symbolizing it with the rose, one of the oldest signs of secrecy.

Given the ubiquity of metaphor in everyday conversations, Lakoff and Johnson renamed many kinds of abstract ideas *conceptual metaphors*, defining them as generalized metaphorical thought formulas that underlie the abstractions.[8] For example, the expression "Love is sweet" is really a token of something more general, namely the conceptual metaphor *love-as-gustation*. This is why we can also say that *love* is *bitter, sour, spicy*, among other gustatory adjectives. All these are specific *linguistic metaphors*, which are tied to the generic conceptual metaphor, *love-as-gustation*. Without going into the details of conceptual metaphor theory, suffice it to say that when we speak about something abstract, such as love, we are likely utilizing a metaphorical system of meaning that is based on connecting experientially and historically significant ideas. So, one could hypothesize that the *love-as-gustation* conceptual metaphor might derive from the gustatory and affective responses that lip-kissing might evoke, or else the sensation that various gustatory flavors produce in us. The metaphor thus connects our physiological reactions (World 1) to a feeling (World 2) in terms of language (World 3). Now, whether or not it can be shown empirically that kissing is the source of this conceptual metaphor or not, it certainly can be inferred. Romantic kissing as we know it today originates in the chivalric code and it is in this period that metaphors connecting love to gustation also emerge.[9]

Conceptual metaphors link mental impressions to experiences and resemblances, permitting us not only to recognize patterns within certain bodily sensations, but also to anticipate their consequences and to make inferences about them. Thus, the choice of a taste to describe romance suggests that the source domain enlisted in talking about love was not chosen in an arbitrary fashion, but derived from the experience of events. A 1955 study by the Gestalt psychologist Solomon Asch actually suggested that metaphors of love and sex in several phylogenetically-unrelated languages used the same sensory source adjectives (*warm, cold, heavy*, etc.), although the particular meaning of specific items varied from language to language.[10] For example, he found that *hot* stood for *rage* in Hebrew (much like the rage felt by Gianciotto or Medea), *enthusiasm* in Chinese (similar to the one experienced by young lovers), *sexual arousal* in Thai, and *energy* in Hausa. As psychologist Roger Brown aptly commented shortly after the publication of Asch's study, "there is an undoubted kinship of meanings" in different languages that "seem to involve activity and emotional arousal."[11] This type of research implies that the use of sensory reactions to emotional stimuli, such as love, is part of a general blending system in the brain that amalgamates the two domains into a singular thought unit. Indeed, the only way to convey the feeling of love is through conceptual metaphors. Neural blending may also be the source of love symbolism. The color *red*, for instance, suggests "blood" and thus "vitality," and thus a heart metaphor. This is why a *red heart* is commonly used as a symbol of love and passion.

As the work of Zoltan Kövecses has shown abundantly, there is no better way to understand and communicate love than through metaphor.[12] So, returning to the *love-as-a-physical-reaction* metaphor, we can see its traces in expressions such as "to have *crush*," "to see someone as *hot*," "*burning* love" (a song by Elvis Presley), "light my *fire*" (a song by the Doors), "an old *flame*," "*steamy* love or sex," and "*melting* in someone's arms." The sensation of *falling* is the source of another common conceptual love metaphor, as can be seen in expressions such as: "*falling* in love," "*tumble* head over heels," "her look *knocked* me out," "I was *swept* off my feet." The concept of *love-as-a-binding-connective-force*, and its opposite, can be seen in expressions such as: "*close* lovers," "they have *drifted apart*," "they are *joined* together by love," "*breaking up* is hard to do" (a Neil Sedaka song), "they just *split up*." Of course, if a "break-up" occurs then there could be ways of reconnecting, as metaphorical expressions such as the following indicate: "they're love can be *fixed* or *repaired*," "*mending* their relationship." "*patching* things up." Similar conceptual metaphors are found in other languages, as Kövecses has documented, suggesting a kind of common grasp of the love feeling. The study of love metaphors may, in fact, provide a clue reaching into the origins of love itself in opposition to sex. The *love-as-a-heat-sensation* metaphor, for example, is arguably a cognitive strategy for connecting love and sex biologically and emotionally. When the type of "heat" becomes intense during sex, we tend to speak of love in terms of *fireworks* and *explosions*, and when it *dies down* in terms of ways to *reignite* it within the body.

The metaphorical link between *love* and *insanity* suggests that the love feeling alters our normal state of mind, thrusting us temporarily into madness. This is an ancient metaphorical theme, and can be found in texts ranging from the *Kama Sutra* to medieval love poetry where it appears regularly. In *A Midsummer Night's Dream*, Shakespeare describes Theseus, the Duke of Athens, as "The lover, the lunatic and the poet" (V:i). Common expressions such as "I am *crazy* about her," "I have *lost my mind* over him," "I am *mad* about her" are based on the same theme. The likely source of this metaphor is that love instills emotional chaos into one's life. The antidote to madness is to seek solace in magic and astrology. Expressions such as *"enchanted* love," *"star-crossed* lovers," "love is written in the *stars*," and others show how much we think of love as a metaphysical, and hence magical, force, rather than just a physical one. Other common metaphorical constructs for love include *love-as-a game* ("their love has always been a *chess match*"), *love-as-sport* ("their love is a *marathon*"), and *love-as-a-commodity* ("can't *buy* me love, a song by the Beatles").

The list of conceptual metaphors for love is truly astounding, confirming that we have been fascinated and obsessed by this feeling since the dawn of history. The counterpart of metaphor is irony, a cognitive strategy by which a concept such as *love* is highlighted through opposition, antithesis, or antonymy. An ironic work, such as Woody Allen's *Everything You Wanted to Know About Sex* (1972), would hardly be interpreted as a serious treatment of love. It is an ironic depiction of the ludicrous neurotic behaviors of people preoccupied with love when it is deconstructed to sex. Irony is a means of criticizing the very concepts we hold dear, forming a semiotic counterpart with metaphor as a way of understanding something in a contrastive and often ludicrous way.

Cultural Metaphors

Metaphorical reasoning is intrinsically intertwined with social and cultural phenomena of all kinds, as discussed above. Take again the *love-as-a-sweet-taste* metaphor in English. The manifestations of this concept do not stop at the level of language ("my *sweetheart*," "our *honeymoon*", etc.); they are also evident in specific kinds of symbolic and ritualistic practices. These can be called, simply, cultural metaphors. As mentioned, these include giving chocolates to a loved one on Valentine's Day, symbolizing matrimonial love at a wedding ceremony with a cake, and others. Wherever the same conceptual metaphor is used, the same cultural manifestations appear in different societies. For instance, in Chagga, a Bantu language of Tanzania, comparable cultural practices exist because the language possesses the same conceptual metaphor. In that culture, the man is perceived to be the *eater* and the woman his *sweet food*, as can be detected in expressions that mean, in translated form, "Does she *taste* sweet?" "She *tastes* sweet as sugar honey".[13]

Metaphors are thus guides to a culture's mindset and to it past. As the literary critic Northrop Frye aptly pointed out, one cannot penetrate western literature or art without having been exposed, directly or indirectly, to the original Biblical stories.[14] These provide the sources for many of the metaphorical concepts we use today for judging human actions and offering advice, bestowing upon everyday life a kind of implicit metaphysical meaning and value. Proverbs are cultural metaphors that people employ to provide sound practical advice when it is required in certain situations. In the case of love, the following proverbs and sayings impart perspective and wisdom related to common experiences of love:

Absence makes the heart grow fonder (indicating that when the loved one is far away the love feeling intensifies)

A loving heart is the truest wisdom (Charles Dickens, indicating that love and wisdom are interconnected)

Love will find a way (suggesting that sooner or later people will experience love in some form)

Love is composed of a single soul inhabiting two bodies (Aristotle, implying that love is binding force)

A truly insightful tradition of love proverbs comes from African languages, as Kovie Biakolo has pointed out.[15] The following list is instructive in this regard:

You know who you love but you can't know who loves you (Nigeria, implying that love may not be reciprocal)

Where there is love, there is no darkness (Burundi, suggesting that love is a key to understanding and enlightenment)

The one who loves, will love you with your dirt (Uganda, indicating that when someone is in love, they will accept the loved one unconditionally)

Love doesn't rely on physical features (Lesotho, corresponding somewhat to English "love is in the eye of the beholder" or "love is blind")

Love is a despot that spares no one (Namibia, implying that everyone will fall in love, sooner or later, constituting an irresistible emotional force)

The quarrel of lovers is the renewal of love (Morocco, indicating that conflicts between lovers are qualitatively different from other kinds of conflicts and common in courtship and marriage)

A letter from the heart can be read on the face (Kenya, referring to the effects of love on people's facial appearance and demeanor)

Love doesn't listen to rumors (Ghana, implying that the person in love does not pay attention to gossip and hearsay when it comes to matters of the heart)

Love, like rain, does not choose the grass on which it falls (South Africa, suggesting that love is a natural force that falls upon people whether they want it or not)

Every culture has similar proverbs, aphorisms, and sayings. They constitute a remarkable code of practical knowledge that anthropologists call folk wisdom. Indeed, the very concept of *wisdom* implies the ability to apply proverbial language meaningfully to a situation. The Bible contains many sayings and proverbs that relate to love and marriage. Below is a small sampling:

May your fountain be blessed, and…may you ever be intoxicated with her love. (Proverbs 5:18–19)

If I speak in the tongues of men or of angels, but do not have love, I am only a resounding gong or a clanging cymbal. If I have the gift of prophecy and can fathom all mysteries and all knowledge, and if I have a faith that can move mountains, but do not have love, I am nothing. If I give all I possess to the poor and give over my body to hardship that I may boast, but do not have love, I gain nothing. (1 Corinthians 13:1–3)

Love is patient, love is kind. It does not envy, it does not boast, it is not proud. It does not dishonor others, it is not self-seeking, it is not easily angered, it keeps no record of wrongs. Love does not delight in evil but rejoices with the truth. It always protects, always trusts, always hopes, always perseveres. Love never fails. (1 Corinthians 13:4–8)

Love must be sincere. Hate what is evil; cling to what is good. Be devoted to one another in love. Honor one another above yourselves. (Romans 12:9–10)

Be completely humble and gentle; be patient, bearing with one another in love. Make every effort to keep the unity of the Spirit through the bond of peace. (Ephesians 4:2–3)

All proverbs are based on conceptual metaphors that connect language to belief systems, philosophies, and cultural codes. For instance, in the Proverbs 5:18–19 quote above, love is conceptualized as "intoxication," connecting it (in all likelihood) to wine and how it can cause someone to lose control of their faculties or behavior. In the 1 Corinthians 13:1–3 quote, love is something that we *have*, that is, possess within us and which is the source of truth and meaning. In the 1 Corinthians 13:4–8 citation, love is portrayed as a person who possesses Christian values—it is patient, kind, hopeful, etc. Personification is one of the most basic of all metaphorical processes, underlying mythic structure. The mythic personification of natural events, for example, is an instinctual metaphorical strategy for making sense of things. The warming of the ocean surface off the western coast of South America that occurs every 4 to 12 years when upwelling of cold, nutrient-rich water is not caused by a being. Nevertheless, we ascribe it to El Niño, "the little one" in Spanish. This makes the climatological condition much more understandable in concrete terms. Although people do not think of El Niño as a person, they nonetheless find it convenient to blame "him" for certain weather repercussions. Similarly, the personification of love in the proverb above allows us to separate it from the inner complex of emotions, giving it life as a virtuous person and then describing how such a person would act and behave. A similar set of virtues associated with love are described in the remaining two proverbs (Romans 12:9–10 and Ephesians 4:2–3).

The foregoing discussion was intended to show that metaphor is the unconscious strategy we use to interconnect domains of concepts and experiences into increasingly layered orders of meaning—layers upon layers of metaphors. One metaphor suggests another, which suggests another, and so on. The central feature of human thinking is the fluid application of existing concepts to new situations. The result is an interconnected system of meanings that inform us about everyday life and its basis in cultural history interacting with creative innovation. Michel Foucault characterized this network as an endless "interrelated fabric" in which the boundaries of meanings are never clear-cut.[16] Every single metaphor is caught up in a system of references to other metaphors, to codes, and to texts; it is a node within a network of distributed signs. As soon as one questions that unity, it loses its self-evidence; it indicates itself. To extract meaning from a sign, code, or text, therefore, one must have knowledge of this network and of the metaphors that constitute it.

Consider again the meaning of the *rose* as a symbol for *love* as expressed in the *love-as-a-rose* conceptual metaphor. The *rose* is connected to three concrete source domains—*smell, color,* and *plants*—domains that also deliver the concept of *love* in discourse ("There relation has the *smell* of romance"; Their love is a *rosy* one indeed"; "Their love *blossomed* a while back"). The *rose* concept is the product of a cultural metaphorical process, compressing all domains and historical forms into one symbolic artifact. It is born in the symbolism of the rose as both an emblem of secrecy and feminine beauty. It is the result of what Charles Pierce called an *abduction*—a tendency to link concepts to each other, not by a pure flight of fancy, but because they entail or implicate each other.[17] Thus, the concept of *love* implicates the concept of a *rose* and, vice versa, *roses* implicate *love*. This type of "bidirectional" entailment is the essence of metaphor.[18] At a cognitive level, the color associated with the rose, *red*, is itself a metaphorical source for understanding love, as we have seen, which we have probably extrapolated from observing the flushing of the face that often typifies love situations.

The semiotic structure of metaphor indicates that we blend sensations, ideas, cultural images, etc. into a singular form. In psychology, *associationism* is the theory that the mind comes to form concepts by combining simple, irreducible elements through mental connection. One of the first to recognize this feature of the mind was Aristotle, who identified four strategies by which associations are forged: by similarity (an orange and a lemon), difference (hot and cold), contiguity in time (sunrise and a rooster's crow), and contiguity in space (a cup and saucer). British empiricist philosophers John Locke and David Hume saw sensory perception as the underlying factor in guiding the associative process; that is, things that are perceived to be similar or contiguous in time or space are associated to each other; those that are not are kept distinct.[19] In the later nineteenth century, the early psychologists, guided by the principles enunciated by James Mill in his *Analysis of the Phenomena of the Human Mind*, studied experimentally how subjects made associations.[20] In addition to Aristotle's original four strategies, they found that factors such as intensity, inseparability, and repetition played a role in associative processes: for example, arms are associated with bodies because they are inseparable from them; rainbows are associated with rain because of repeated observations of the two as co-occurring phenomena; etc. Metaphor seems to encompass all these associative mechanisms, and much more, since it also delves into happenstance historical events. It is hopeless to talk about love without recourse to these mechanisms. As James Edie has insightfully remarked, it is "impossible to understand the human mind or human behavior except by making a metaphorical detour."[21]

The role of irony to deconstruct our love metaphors was mentioned briefly above. It is relevant to note that Lakoff and Johnson see irony, as well as metonymy, as cognitively different from metaphor. Metonymy involves using the part to stand for the whole. Particularly productive in love portrayals is the metonymic concept of the face as a conveyor of the body-in-love sign system, discussed in the previous chapter. The concept of *person* itself derives from the theater and the wearing of masks. The Latin term for "cast of characters" is *dramatis personae*, literally, "the persons of the drama," which betrays the theatrical-metonymic origin of our concept of personhood. *Persona* was the mask in Greek theater. After time, it became associated with the character of the mask-wearer. The face-in-love is a type of "love mask," which reveals the inner feelings prompted by love.

Love Poetry

Poetry is the natural language of love. This is not a mere cliché; it is a historical fact. Cultures across the world and across time have employed poetic verse to represent and convey the rhythms and internal feelings of love through metaphorical words and their rhyming patterns. As discussed previously, the Roman poet Catullus begs his lover Lesbia poetically to give him countless kisses until he loses count in a "kissing maze." The twentieth century poet E. E. Cummings describes a woman's "profound and fragile lips" as the path to his soul. From time immemorial, we have resorted to such poetic speech to literally make sense of love. The late-seventeenth-early-eighteenth-century Italian philosopher, Giambattista Vico, saw poetry as the original form of language.[22] We are all born poets, Vico suggested, using our senses to link things together into holistic ideas through poetic metaphors. It is this "linking through sense" capacity that makes poetry so powerful.

The origin of modern love poetry can be traced back to the chivalric code and especially the troubadours, a group of poet-musicians who flourished in southern France and northern Italy in the 1200s. They composed their love poetry in local languages such as Provençal, rather than in Latin, which was the official language of Europe in that era, indicating that they aimed to reach common folk, not just aristocrats. They called their poems *cansi d'amor* ("songs of love"), since they were set to music. In the typical *canso*, the troubadour praises the lady of his dreams as the model of virtue, and to whom he dedicates his heart forever. This intense pining over love influenced subsequent poets, remaining a model for love ballads to this day which, like the troubadour's songs, are about love at first sight, first kisses, heartbreak, betrayal, and passion. Below are three lines from a troubadour *canso*, written by Guillaume IX, Duke of Aquitaine and Gascony and Count of Poitou circa 1086[23]:

> If shortly I do not have the love of my good lady,
> I will die, by St. Gregory's head!
> Unless she kisses me in her room or under a tree.

In this marvelous poem, Guillaume emphasizes the redeeming effects of his beloved's love. This image of the troubadour singing to his paramour, perhaps under her balcony, was captured powerfully by Giuseppe Verdi in his great opera *Il Trovatore* (1853), with its gloomy and fateful melancholy, recalling the ill-fated love affairs of the troubadours and, by extension, the power of love to override even the desire for life, which, without love would be meaningless.

At about the same time as the troubadours, in Italy a new poetic style known as the *dolce stil nuovo* ("sweet new style") emerged. In it, women were extolled as *angeli* ("angels"). The style also broke away from the use of Latin as the language of writing, adopting the emerging vernaculars, or spoken languages of the people, emphasizing the role of love in bringing about social changes. The new style was at first connected to the so-called Sicilian School, which emerged at the court of Emperor Frederick II, who ruled in the city of Palermo during the first half of the 1200s. Frederick brought together intellectuals and poets into his court, urging them to write in the Sicilian vernacular. All the poems were about love without social strictures, prefiguring the Paolo and Francesca story. The School ceased to exist in 1226, but the poetry in *dolce stil nuovo* style spread to other parts of Italy. The same *woman-as-angelic* metaphor is found, of course, in the ancient love goddess myths and in the Bible and other sacred texts, where women are both revered as spiritual gifts to humanity and condemned as sources of temptation. In all this, the female point of view was not lacking, as we saw in the opening chapter with the works of Christine de Pizan. Other well-known poets of the *dolce stil nuovo* era were Marie de France, who lived circa 1160 to 1215 and Bietris de Romans who lived in the early thirteenth century. Both wrote in the courtly love style, extolling love as a spiritual force. Bietris was a *trobairitz*, the name used to designate a female troubadour, who actually composed her songs for a certain Lady Maria, praising the love they had for each other, which was, at the very least, unusual for the era. As she wrote in one of her songs, for her, Maria possessed "All good things one could ask of a woman".[24]

It is the poetry of Dante in the early 1300s that best exemplified the *dolce stil nuovo* movement. In one of his most powerful works, *La vita nuova* ("The New Life"), Dante states that the single life-altering event of his youth was his fortuitous meeting with Beatrice, a young woman with whom he fell desperately in love, becoming his muse. The work, which was written not long after Beatrice died and which had deeply affected Dante, is a declaration of his ultimate resolve to write a work that would be a worthy monument to her memory. That work turned out to be his masterpiece, *The Divine Comedy*. The love poetry of the medieval period led to the madrigal of the Renaissance, starting in the early 1400s, which became popular among all social classes. Madrigals were performed in public squares throughout Italy.[25] The greatest composer of madrigals was undoubtedly Claudio Monteverdi, who greatly influenced the emergence of opera as an autonomous musical-dramatic genre. Monteverdi's madrigals were hauntingly melodic, leading to the *bel canto* ("beautiful song") style of opera that developed a century or so later.

The Medieval and Renaissance poetic traditions have left their permanent traces on the language of love. Indeed, some of the best-known lines that discuss love come from poetry, leaving their conceptual traces on groupthink. Below is a sampling:

How do I love thee? Let me count the ways. I love thee to the depth and breadth and height my soul can reach. (Elizabeth Barrett Browning, *How Do I Love Thee?*)

I wonder by my troth, what thou and I did, till we loved? (John Donne, *The Good-Morrow*)

She walks in Beauty, like the night / Of Cloudless climes and starry skies; / And all that's best of dark and bright / Meet in her aspect and her eyes. (Lord Byron, *She Walks in Beauty*)

i carry your heart with me (i carry it in my heart) i am never without it (anywhere i go you go, my dear; and whatever is done by only me is your doing, my darling). (E. E. Cummings, *i carry your heart with me*)

That I did always love / I bring thee Proof / That till I loved / I never lived. (Emily Dickinson, *That I Did Always Love*)

You were born together, and together you shall be forever more. You shall be together when the white wings of death scatter your days. (Khalil Gibran, *Love One Another*)

The poem by Browning implies the importance of love for understanding our very nature. Donne's poem conveys the sense that love is not subject to the constraints of time, and is inscribed in everyone's destiny, so that our life before love is barely a fleeting memory. Byron's poem is based on the *light-dark* opposition, with the former indicating the illumination that comes from loving and the latter the darkness that exists without it. The poem by Cummings is grounded on two conceptual metaphors: *love-occurs-in-the heart* and *love-is-a-portable-emotion* suggesting that love is not bound to any specific situation but transcends all physical constraints. Dickinson's marvelous little poem bespeaks of love as destiny and its power to infuse life with meaning. Khalil Gibran's poem is a paean to the ability of love to join lovers together in an eternal embrace.

One of the greatest collections of love poetry of all time is *The Rubaiyat*, by the medieval Persian poet and mathematician Omar Khayyam. The *Rubaiyat* is a kind of cryptogram, since it is highly allegorical and metaphorical, much like complex riddles. The poem begins at the break of New Year's Day, which in Khayyam's time meant the vernal equinox. The poet uses metaphorical love images connected with the spring season, such as grapes, roses, the nightingale, and the garden which lead him to ponder the mystery of life and its connection to love. The poet bids his companion lover to follow him into the wilderness along with a book of verses and a loaf of bread, reminding us that life is ephemeral and that we should thus seek truth in the simple things of life before it ends. It is love which transcends physical life giving us a glimpse into the sense of eternity that we all desire.

Needless to say, since at least the nineteenth century, poetry has branched out into other realms, from existentialism and surrealism to nihilism and beyond. The movement called *Symbolism*, which originated in France in the latter part of the century, greatly influenced the evolution of modern love poetry. The Symbolists believed that the world is an illusion. They used metaphorical images to suggest a connection between the visible and invisible worlds as they unfolded within the imagination. The first major Symbolist was Charles Baudelaire, whose 1857 collection, *Les fleurs du mal* (The Flowers of Evil) established the groundwork for modern poetry. In the work, love is carnal and physically real, as can be seen in several of its stanzas:

> Rare wines or opium are less a prize
> Than your moist lips where love struts its pavane;
> When my lusts move towards you in caravan
> My ennuis drink from cisterns of your eyes.
> …
> Ah, then, o my beauty, explain to the worms
> Who cherish your body so fine,
> That I am the keeper for corpses of love
> Of the form, and the essence divine!

In the first stanza, the sexual allure of the lips, symbolizing the kiss as a dance, the pavane, are an antidote to his inner *ennuis*, inviting the poet to become involved lustfully. In the end, everything dies, as the second stanza emphasizes. Under ground, it is the worms who are attracted to the body, not a lover, and the only "essence divine" is the corpse. Clearly, this is a long way from the exquisite love poetry of the courtly period and the *dolce stil nuovo*. Poetry was turning away from idealism and veering towards realism and an inherent sense of nihilism. With many styles and movements, modern poetry has reflected the fragmented psyche that the contemporary world has engendered. But this is nothing new. Even in antiquity, as we saw in the opening chapter, poetry was used to understand the human condition in its fragmented nature. The Greek epic poems, the *Iliad* and the *Odyssey*, tell of the deeds of heroes in battle with other humans, nature, and divine forces. The *Iliad* describes events in the last year of the Trojan War, which was fought between Greece and the city of Troy. The *Odyssey* tells of the adventures of Odysseus, king of Ithaca, on his return home after having fought for Greece in the Trojan War. In both, the tales of love, betrayal, and romance, leading to crimes of passion, tell ultimately of the fatality of the human condition. The difference in the case of modern poetry, is that it tells not of fatality, but of futility.

However our sense that love conquers all—to use yet another cliché— has not disappeared, having been adopted by the world of popular music, where the idealism of love is still fervent and the power of passion still vibrant. Popular music has always focused on romance, on break-ups, and on what is called within the country genre, "hurtin' music." It has continued in an unbroken chain the metaphors of the *dolce stil nuovo* and the troubadours. Among the most common are the *donna-angelo* (angel-woman), the *heart*, and the *madness* metaphors, as the sampling of popular song titles below shows:

Angel metaphor
 "Earth Angel" (The Penguins, 1954)
 "Teen Angel" (Mark Denning, 1960)
 "Pretty Little Angel Eyes" (Curtis Lee, 1961)
 "Send Me an Angel" (Real Life, 1983)
 "Angel eyes" (Tony Bennett, 1992)

Heart metaphor
 "How Can You Mend A Broken Heart?" (Bee Gees, 1971)
 "Total Eclipse of the Heart" (Bonnie Tyler, 1983)
 "Listen To Your Heart" (Roxette, 1989)
 "Achy Breaky Heart" (Billy Ray Cyrus, 1992)
 "My Heart Will Go On" (Celine Dion, 1997)

Madness metaphor
"Crazy" (Patsy Cline, 1961)
"Undun" (The Guess Who, 1969)
"Crazy Love" (Poco, 1978)
"Going Out of My Head" (Fatboy Slim, 1997)
"You Drive Me Crazy" (Britney Spears, 1999)

The sense that poetry is the natural the language of love was brought out powerfully by the heartbreaking 1994 movie *Il postino* (The Postman), directed by Michael Radford and Massimo Troisi. The movie deals with a simple postman who delivers letters to the Chilean poet Pablo Neruda, while living in Italy. The shy and simple postman is deeply in love, but does not know how to communicate his feelings to his beloved. So, one day he asks Neruda to help him write poetry. Neruda tells him, rather appropriately, "walk on the shore and the metaphors will come to you." They do and the *postino* comes up with the words that reflect his inner feelings. The movie seems to claim that the chivalric code is still the only meaningful one in our understanding of love, no matter what modern-day skeptics might think.

Love Mythologies

There is a folk Italian love song, originating in the Calabria region, which starts off with the following verse: "Our first love is wonderful, but our second one is even more wonderful" (*Quant'è bello il primo amore, il secondo è più bello ancora*). As the song suggests, the experience of a first love becomes an indelible part of our memory system. But, as the song also wisely suggests, this may not always hold as a principle of romance, asserting that love may not be restricted to one, and only one, paramour. The song is thus partially deconstructive of the myth of idealistic first love, suggesting that love may both enthrall and disappoint us. More significantly, in its allusive subtext is the advice to "let love go," otherwise we will become obsessed by it, and it will ruin us or adversely affect our life.

Many of the original love myths revolve around the same warning. These deal with both love's inspiration alongside its sorrowful and destiny-altering sides. The story of Orpheus and Eurydice, two of the first hopeless lovers of mythic history, encapsulates this dualism. Orpheus was a handsome musician who was unrivaled among mortals for his attractiveness and musical talent. The story goes that he traveled to the underworld to retrieve his dead wife, Eurydice. No mortal had ever entered the underworld. Moved by Orpheus' music, Hades, the ruler of the underworld, brought Eurydice back to life on the condition that Orpheus not look at her until they reached the upper world. But the forlorn lover could not resist, taking a peek at her just before stepping out into the world, making Eurydice vanish. Heart-broken, Orpheus started to wander alone in the wilderness, singing sorrowfully about Eurydice, until he was killed by a band of Thracian women, who cut off his head and threw it into the river, where it continued to sing for his beloved Eurydice.

The Greek story of Acontius, a young man from Ceos, who fell in love with Cydippe emphasizes the inevitability of love's self-fulfilling prophecies, much like our belief in the predictions of astrologers or fortune tellers. The story is told by Callimachus in one of his poems and constitutes the theme of two of Ovid's *Heroides*. Acontius threw an apple at Cydippe, on which he had written cleverly "I swear by the temple of Artemis that I shall marry Acontius," so that Cydippe would read it aloud, unaware that this amounted to an oath of marriage. As a result she reacted with contempt, rejecting Acontius' clever ruse. She was betrothed more than once thereafter, but each time became sick just before the wedding was to take place. An oracle declared that the cause of these maladies was the wrath of the offended goddess Artemis, whereupon Cydippe was impelled to marry Acontius.

The story of Layla extols devotion and describes how love can shatter our sense of order. It was written as a narrative poem by the twelfth-century Persian poet, Nizami Ganjavi, paralleling both the Paolo and Francesca and Romeo and Juliet legendary tales. It tells of the story of Layla and Qays, who fall inexorably in love with each other, but they are denied marriage by her father. Qays becomes obsessed with her, to the point that he is renamed *Majnun*, meaning "insane," "possessed." The poem is based on the real life of a young man called Qays during the Umayyad era in the seventh century. He had indeed fallen in love with Layla, wooing her with his poetry, but his marriage proposal was denied by her father, as in Ganjavi's poem. Qays became crazed with grief and fled into the desert where he would wander in the wilderness and write poetry with a stick in the sand. Eventually, Layla became ill and died and Qays was later found dead at the grave of his beloved Layla.

One of the best known of all the love myths is the story of Pygmalion, a sculptor and king of Cyprus. Pygmalion loathed all women, so he decided to carve the "perfect woman" out of marble, calling her Galatea. He fell deeply in love with his own creation, dressing the sculpted figure and speaking to it with words of love. During Aphrodite's annual festival, Pygmalion went to her altar and implored her to turn Galatea into a real flesh and blood woman. The goddess heard his heartfelt plea and when Pygmalion returned home and kissed Galatea, she became alive. The couple instantly fell in love and had a child named Paphos. This tale has intrigued many writers, from the Roman poet Ovid, who retold the story in his *Metamorphoses*,[26] to George Bernard Shaw, who turned into it into a play, *Pygmalion* (1913), which tells how an English gentleman (a professor of phonetics) transforms a poor ill-bred girl into an elegant lady by teaching her to act and speak with proper grammar and pronunciation.[27] The musical comedy *My Fair Lady* (1956) is based on Shaw's play.

Two of the greatest love myths, based on the same kind of fatalism expressed in the Calabrian folk song, come from the medieval period—the story of Lancelot and Guinevere du Lac and (of course) Romeo and Juliet. The former is a classic tale of ideal love filled with intrigue and dreadful consequences. Guinevere was the wife of the legendary King Arthur. She appears for the first time in the twelfth-century *Historia* cycle of Arthurian romances by English chronicler Geoffrey of Monmouth. It was, however, the French poet Chrétien de Troyes who introduced the story of the tragic love affair between Guinevere and Lancelot to the world.[28] After marrying Arthur, Guinevere is smitten by Lancelot, a handsome knight of the court in Camelot. Their secret love affair eventually brings about the unraveling of Camelot and the downfall of Arthur. The first encounter between the two star-crossed lovers is actually orchestrated by Lancelot's friend, Sir Galahad, and is recorded by de Troyes as follows: "And the queen sees that the knight dares not do more, so she takes him by the chin and kisses him in front of Galahad for quite a long time."[29]

The story of Romeo and Juliet is so well known that it would be trivial to recount it here; moreover, it has already been discussed briefly in the opening chapter. It is still important to emphasize that it is *the* iconic story of star-crossed lovers and of true love as an unattainable ideal in mortal life. According to the Shakespearean version, the lovers belonged to two rival clans, the Capulets and the Montagues. Despite opposition from the families, they tied the wedding knot with the help of Romeo's friend, Friar Lawrence. Unaware of his daughter's marriage, Juliet's father decided to marry her off to Paris. Friar Lawrence advised Juliet to agree misleadingly to the marriage, since on the wedding day she would drink a harmless potion prepared by him that others would think was poison. The potion would only put her into a temporary deep sleep, not kill her. People would believe that she had died; and a little later Romeo would come to rescue her. Juliet agreed. But the plan went awry, since Romeo was not informed in time about it. So, when he heard about his sweetheart's death, he ended up taking his own life to join her in the afterlife. When Juliet awoke, discovering what had actually happened, she also committed suicide, uniting with him forever.

By revisiting the ancient love myths, we can learn a lot about how we grasp the meaning of love. A direct descendant of the mythic tradition is the fairytale, which is invariably about the power of love to conquer all, at least in the world of fantasy and the imagination. The tales take place, in fact, in a fantasy world where magic and the supernatural effects of love reign supreme. The hero or heroine is put through a great trial and, with magical assistance from fairies, secures a romantic partner. Such stories begin with "Once upon a time" and end with "And they lived happily ever after," formulas that imbue them with a sense of eternity and transcendental meaning. We call the latter a "fairytale ending" to this day, implying that love, unfortunately, is never really consummated in the same way in the real world, remaining a topic of myths, stories, and other imaginative artifacts.

A fairy, in folklore, is a diminutive supernatural creature who has a human form and lives in an imaginary region called a fairyland. She intervenes in human affairs, in order to help humans achieve their dreams. The sirens in Homer's *Odyssey* are fairies, and a number of the heroes in the *Iliad*, have nymph-like fairy lovers. The gandharvas (celestial singers and musicians) of Sanskrit poetry were fairies, as were the hathors (female genies) of Egyptian myth. In European literature, fairies appear in such works as *The Faerie Queene* by Edmund Spenser, *Tales of Mother Goose* by Charles Perrault, *Grimm's Fairytales*, by the brothers Jacob and Wilhelm Grimm, and *Irish Fairytales* by William Butler Yeats. The fairies are both loving and capricious. The quintessential cinema fairy is Disney's Tinkerbell, who tried to kill Peter Pan's pal Wendy in a jealous rage. She is both tender and dangerous, gentle and obsessive, like any love fairy of the past.

Epilogue

We hardly ever realize how much the language of love is embedded in our everyday discourse and in out classic stories and proverbs. What would human life be without it, as many philosophers and poets have asked? English writer William Makepeace Thackeray phrased it aptly as follows, "It is best to love wisely, no doubt: but to love foolishly is better than not to be able to love at all."[30] Our need for love is the reason why the famous lovers of history have been etched permanently into our imagination, transcending time: Orpheus and Eurydice, Samson and Delilah, Guinevere and Lancelot, Paolo and Francesca, Romeo and Juliet, among many others. Our love myths, metaphors, and poems have left us with cultural traditions and practices that continue to resonate within us to this day, including the giving of roses as symbolic of love and the giving of chocolates at Valentine's.

Understanding how love, life, and destiny are intertwined is imprinted into the words, metaphors, and stories that we have created about love. We still enjoy reading about idealized romance, in the same way that ancient people probably liked reading about Orpheus and Eurydice and medieval people about love affairs between Lancelot and Guinevere or Paolo and Francesca. Starting around the 1100s the romance stories started to spread, gaining wide popularity. They were, in fact, called "romances" because they dealt with combat, adventure, intrigue, courtship, and love, legitimate or otherwise. The stories about King Arthur and the Knights of the Round Table were among the most popular of these, remaining so to this day, because they dealt not only with adventure but with the passions of love. Centuries later, Horace Walpole's 1874 novel, *The Castle of Otranto*, gave the romantic story that he inherited from this tradition a bit of twist, introducing the first Gothic romance, a genre that revolved around mystery, terror, the supernatural, and ill-fated love. A romance story that does not include a kiss at its core would be an oxymoron. The stories of star-crossed lovers embracing passionately, and promising to remain united forever all start with the kiss. Similarly, stories of love triangles and of betrayal all start with a "fatal" kiss—as we shall see in the next chapter.

Notes

1. George Lakoff and Mark Johnson, *Metaphors We Live By* (Chicago: University of Chicago Press, 1980), p. 3.
2. Franz Boas, *Race, Language, and Culture* (New York: Free Press, 1940).
3. Marissa A. Harrison and Jennifer C. Shortall, "Women and Men in Love: Who Really Feels It and Says It First," *The Journal of Social Psychology* 151 (2011): 727–736.
4. Lakoff and Johnson, *Metaphors We Live By*, op. cit.
5. Aristotle's discussions of metaphor are found in his *Rhetoric: The Works of Aristotle*, W. D. Ross (ed.) (Oxford: Clarendon Press, 1952); and *Poetics: The Works of Aristotle*, W. D. Ross (ed.) (Oxford: Clarendon Press, 1952).
6. Howard R. Pollio, Jack M. Barlow, Harold J. Fine, and Marilyn R. Pollio, *The Poetics of Growth: Figurative Language in Psychology, Psychotherapy, and Education* (Hillsdale, NJ: Lawrence Erlbaum Associates, 1977).
7. This is discussed in Marcel Danesi, *The Origins of the Kiss*, op. cit.
8. Lakoff and Johnson, *Metaphors We Live By*, op. cit.

9. Marcel Danesi, *The Origins of the Kiss*, op. cit.; Nicholas Perella, *The Kiss Sacred and Profane*; op. cit.

10. Solomon Asch, "On the Use of Metaphor in the Description of Persons," in H. Werner (ed.), *On Expressive Language*, pp. 86–94 (Worcester: Clark University Press, 1950).

11. Roger W. Brown, *Words and Things* (New York: The Free Press 1958), p. 146.

12. Zoltan Kövecses, *Metaphors of Anger, Pride, and Love: A Lexical Approach to the Structure of Concepts* (Amsterdam: John Benjamins, 1986); *The Language of Love: The Semantics of Passion in Conversational English* (London: Associated University Presses, 1988); *Emotion Concepts* (New York: Springer, 1990).

13. Michele Emantian, "Metaphor and the Expression of Emotion: The Value of Cross-Cultural Perspectives," *Metaphor and Symbolic Activity* 10: 163–182.

14. Northrop Frye, *The Great Code: The Bible and Literature* (Toronto: Academic Press, 1981).

15. Kovie Biakolo, "25 Ancient African Proverbs About Love That Will Make You Rethink Everything," *Thought Catalogue*, December 17, 2014. https://thoughtcatalog.com/kovie-biakolo/2014/12/25-ancient-african-proverbs-about-love-that-will-make-you-rethink-everything/.

16. Michel Foucault, *The Archeology of Knowledge* (New York: Pantheon, 1972).

17. The notion of abduction is found throughout Peirce's writings, compiled in *Collected Papers of Charles Sanders Peirce*, Vols. 1–8, C. Hartshorne and P. Weiss (eds.) (Cambridge, Mass.: Harvard University Press, 1931–1958).

18. See, for example, Marcel Danesi, "The Bidirectionality of Metaphor," *Poetics Today* 38 (2017): 15–33.

19. John Locke, *An Essay Concerning Humane Understanding* (London: Collins, 1690); David Hume, *An Enquiry Concerning Human Understanding* (Oxford: Clarendon, 1749).

20. James Mill, *Analysis of the Phenomena of the Human Mind* (London: Longmans, 1829).

21. James Edie, *Speaking and Meaning: The Phenomenology of Language* (Bloomington: Indiana University Press, 1976), p. 193.

22. Giambattista Vico, *The New Science*, trans. Thomas H. Bergin and Max Fisch (Ithaca: Cornell University Press, 1984).

23. Guillaume IX, "Farai chansoneta nueva," in *Les Chansons de Guillaume IX*, ed. A. Jeanroy (Paris: Champion, 1927), p. 20.

24. Meg Bogin, *The Women Troubadours* (New York: W. W. Norton & Company, 1980), p. 133.

25. Comprehensive treatments of the madrigal can be found in Alfred Einstein, *The Italian Madrigal* (Princeton: Princeton University Press, 1949) and Iain Fenlon and James Haar, *The Italian Madrigal in the 16th Century: Sources and Interpretation* (Cambridge: Cambridge University Press, 1988).

26. Ovid, *Metamorphoses*, translated by A. D. Melville (Oxford: Oxford University Press, 2009).

27. George Bernard Shaw, *Pygmalion* (London: Penguin, 2013).
28. Chrétien de Troyes, *Arthurian Romances* (Rockville, MD: Wildside Press, 2008).
29. Chrétien de Troyes, *Arthurian Romances*, p. 34.
30. William Makepeace Thackeray, *The History of Pendennis: His Fortunes and Misfortunes, His Friends and His Greatest Enemy* (Boston: Houghton, Miflin, 1850), p. 36.

4

Love Stories

The minute I heard my first love story, I started looking for you.
—Jalaluddin Rumi (1207–1273)

Prologue

Stories of lovers and their escapades are found throughout the literary traditions of all nations, starting in antiquity with myths and tales of forlorn love, jealousy, betrayal, and even murder caused by unrequited love. Cumulatively, these provide a narrative chronicle of the meanings assigned to love by people of all eras and its co-occurrence with lust and carnality. Many insights can thus be gleaned from the relevant romance literature, constituting yet another important semiotic tool for examining how our views of love, including its relation to lust and obsession, have been encoded imaginatively and what this all tells about love itself. Most love stories move us deeply, akin to how powerful melodic music strikes resonant emotional chords within us. To this day, there is nothing more engaging than a story about star-crossed lovers holding hands at night, kissing tenderly and passionately, and promising to remain united to each other forever, no matter what the world thinks. The prototypical romance story is about idealized love, even though it may bring about dire consequences and even end up in crimes of passion. But there are other kinds of love stories that have an opposite terrifying effect on us, because they deal with the darker impulses that are associated with the obsession that love evokes. One could in fact

© The Author(s) 2019
M. Danesi, *The Semiotics of Love*, Semiotics and Popular Culture,
https://doi.org/10.1007/978-3-030-18111-6_4

write an entire history of humanity by selecting and integrating the many love stories of every culture into a cohesive overarching story about the human condition. There are virtually no significant episodes in history that do not involve love in some way.

The narrative blueprint for the romantic love story comes from medieval literature, with tales about Paolo and Francesca, Romeo and Juliet, and Lancelot and Guinevere, which merge historical fact with imaginative fiction. They are essentially *romans à clef*, stories about real life overlaid with the veneer of fiction. One of the most iconic of these tales is the medieval legend of Tristan and Isolde, a *roman* retold over and over in many versions ever since. The basic story tells about the knight Tristan who fell irrevocably in love with the Irish princess Isolde (Iseult), after he drinks a love potion accidentally. Isolde was betrothed to another man—Tristan's uncle, King Mark of Cornwall. An adulterous love affair ensues between Tristan and the princess, driving Mark to seek murderous revenge on them. But the two star-crossed lovers escape to the forest where they live happily ever after. Was it love or lust that brought the two together? It depends on who the storyteller is and what the intent was, as can be seen in different versions of the story. As told by Wolfram von Eschenbach in the early 1200s, the love tryst actually ends with death, not a fairytale ending. Whatever its version, the blueprint of star-crossed lovers whose affair ends in tragedy has had a substantial impact on literature since it first appeared. Its residues can be seen in such modern-day narratives as *Elvira Madigan* (1967), which recounts the real-life story of a famous circus performer named Elvira Madigan who meets a Swedish military officer named Sixten Sparre, who is married with two children. They fall head-over-heels in love with each other and, to avoid repercussions, decide to run away. But because Sixten deserted the army, he cannot secure any job and the couple encounters hardship. With no financial help coming, the couple decide to enjoy a final meal together in the North Forest of Sweden, after which Sparre shoots Elvira and then himself. The cemetery in which the two lovers are buried is still visited by tourists today, in search of the sense of true love that their story continues to inspire.

The love story has embraced all possibilities, not just the classic narrative template of medieval lore. It connects models of romance to relevant social issues of modernity. For example, in *Sunday Bloody Sunday*, a 1971 film about a love triangle between two males and a female, there is a passionate kiss between the two males on screen. It was not the first time that this occurred in a Hollywood film, but it certainly was the first to garner broad social attention, igniting a society-wide debate on love as transcending gender and sexual orientation. The first instance of a same-sex kiss on the silver screen occurred in 1927, when two male soldiers kissed tenderly on the lips in the silent movie, *Wings*, which won Best Picture at the first Academy Awards. No one raised an eyebrow about the scene, probably because kissing in the trenches for reasons of solidarity and camaraderie was common during World War I. Three years later, the first female-to-female mouth kiss was the centerpiece of the movie *Morocco* (1930). Iconic actress Marlene Dietrich wore a man's tuxedo and top hat as a performer in a cabaret club, anticipating subsequent cross-dressing films, such as *La cage aux folles* (1978), blurring the gender lines substantively. The kissing scene comes as she sings *Quand l'Amour* ("When Love"), whence she moves towards the audience, plucking a flower from the hair of an attractive young lady and asking her: "May I have this?" Dietrich then kisses the woman passionately on the mouth to the wild applause of the audience. The scene somehow did not cause much of a stir in America, probably because the nation was undergoing a radical social revolution in more tolerant sexual attitudes. In fact, the movie won several awards including Best Director (Joseph von Sternberg). Today, same-sex romantic kissing has become commonplace on all screens, from movie to computer screens. Films like *Brokeback Mountain* (2005) have succeeded in breaking down the previous gender codes further, showing, if nothing else, that love does indeed transcend sexuality.

Love Fiction

Scholars of literary history regard the eleventh century *Tale of Genji*, by the Japanese baroness Murasaki Shikibu as the first true fictional love story, since it depicts the amorous adventures of an imaginary (not real or legendary) Prince Genji and the staid lives of his subjects. The narrative actually paints a charming picture of Japanese court life in the Heian period. Among its chief features are the penetrating portraits of the women in Prince Genji's life, with their aristocratic refinements and their talents in the arts of music, drawing, and poetry, alongside their secret, yet powerful, amorous feelings. As the work nears its conclusion, the tone becomes more mature and somber, colored by Buddhist insight into the fleeting joys of earthly existence. Fiction did not become a standard literary craft, however, until the publication of Giovanni Boccaccio's *Decameron* (1351–1353), a collection of 100 fictional tales set against the gloomy background of the Black Death, as the bubonic plague that swept through Europe in the fourteenth century was called. To escape an outbreak of the plague, ten friends take refuge in a country villa outside Florence, entertaining one another over ten days with a series of ten stories each, called *novellas*, literally "new things." Many of these are satires about the silliness of sexual encounters and the hypocrisy that often enfolds love trysts.

Novels gained enormous social importance in the succeeding fourteenth and fifteenth centuries. In the midst of the spreading art of the novel, the romance narrative emerged as a staple, tracing its roots to the medieval tales of love, as discussed previously and to be revisited below. In these novels, the plots revolve, as in the medieval tales, around the unattainability of love, which must nonetheless be pursued at any cost to one's life. Once smitten, there is nothing a lover can do, but to follow the call of passion to wherever it may lead. An example is the *Tale of Two Lovers*, written in 1444 by Aeneas Piccolomini, who became Pope Pius II. The novel is replete with erotic imagery, portraying desire as an intrinsic part of love. The plot is set in the city of Siena, revolving around the love affair of a married woman, Lucretia, with the nobleman, Euryalus. At first, the two are unaware that they are deeply in love with each other. They become consciously aware of it after they start a correspondence, which constitutes the main part of the novel—a correspondence in which eroticism and romance are blended seamlessly together. Interestingly, Euryalus begins his first letter by quoting Virgil's famous dictum, "Love conquers all; let us all yield to love."

By the sixteenth century, such stories had become so popular that they caused moral panic among the clergy and the aristocracy; they were, as a result, descried as "Lewd and without decency as to rile the public" by Queen Elizabeth I, who reigned from 1558 to 1603. In the subsequent centuries, love fiction receded to the margins of narrative literature, although within all the novels love always played a role in some way. Its resurgence occurred in the eighteenth and nineteenth centuries, when love was portrayed with psychological realism, although it was still imagined as an ideal to be pursued—no matter what. The best-known novelist in the genre was Jane Austen, who described the subtle complexities of romance with a keen sense of irony about the courtship practices of the era. In her novels, a woman meets and marries an eligible man after a series of ludicrous or ridiculous circumstances. Overcoming these is what leads the lovers to the kind of self-knowledge needed for a serene marriage. In *Pride and Prejudice* (1813), Austen's most famous work, the protagonist Elizabeth Bennet dislikes, at first, the supercilious attitude of Fitzwilliam Darcy, but is nonetheless strongly attracted to him. There is no love at first sight here. Their marriage can only be realized successfully if he humbles his pride and she discards her prejudice. The novels of the Brontë sisters (Emily, Charlotte, and Anne) portray the mystery and fear of love, in Gothic and Romantic ways, as will be discussed below. Love assails psychologically-tormented characters in these works, but it is, nonetheless, the only inner force that may lead them out of their fear and misery, even though it still shatters everyday life and its commodious patterns. The same realistic approach to love and romance was adopted in the twentieth century by Daphne Du Maurier, whose plots are full of mystery and suspense, mirroring the mystery of love itself. In *Rebecca* (1938), Du Maurier paints a powerful portrait of a sensitive young woman disturbed by the memory of her husband's first wife, thus bringing the emotional complexities of love and marriage into sharp modern psychoanalytic focus.

A significant trend in twentieth and twenty-first century love fiction is a "retro" portrayal of love set in the chivalric medieval era. This is evident in the many Harlequin-type romances, television soap operas, and the various idyllic love novels of recent times. These constitute an attempt to revisit the era of courtly love with modern narrative eyes, updating it somewhat, but still retaining the chivalric code blueprint. Alongside this trend is the spread of "chick lit," which forms a counterpart to this type of retro-fiction, starting with the 1997 novel *Bridget Jones's Diary* by Helen Fielding. The plots in these novels revolve around twenty- and thirty-something-year-old women involved in a career in an urban setting, but searching for the "perfect guy." However, if he is not to be found, then it is acceptable to remain unmarried or to even not have a romantic partner at all. Life goes on just the same. This genre constitutes an indirect criticism of traditional courtship and marriage practices, but not of romance per se. TV programs such as *Sex and the City* were products of the same evolving mindset.

Janice Radway argues that reading love stories today, in whatever form they appear, is not a compulsion conditioned by false ideals, but rather a pleasurable activity in itself, above and beyond what critics have to say about them.[1] The romance, she claims, has appeal because it taps into the need for ideal love, an inner force that is inevitable and life-altering. Its pursuit is something we do impulsively, even if we do so in an ersatz way through the narrative medium, and even if it is never totally realized in real life. Fantasy and reality are enmeshed inextricably in our modern love stories, as they have always been.

Fantasy and Reality

The final scene of Disney's 1937 movie, *Snow White and the Seven Dwarfs*, when a prince kisses Snow White, bringing her back to life, is pure fantasy; but its appeal is compelling to this day. The movie is based on an 1810 story by the Brothers Grimm, but differs significantly from it. The main characters in the film are two larger-than-life women—Snow White and the evil queen.

The men, on the other hand, are seven endearing and friendly dwarfs who enthusiastically and cheerfully serve Snow White, catering to her demands, having fallen madly in love with her. Snow White is a ruler of nature and of the heart, recalling the myth of Gaia, or the Earth personified as a goddess who rules over everything and everyone. All respond to Snow White's maternal and loving command, from the dwarfs to the animals in the forest, and even the Prince, who is beckoned to her side by some inner mysterious compulsion. Disney's version of the story emphasizes the fantasy power of love as an unconscious, mythic force in shaping human life.

Disney followed up on the same kind of underlying mythological theme with *Sleeping Beauty* (1959), in which a beautiful princess is again awakened from a deathly slumber by a charming prince with a tender kiss. But the original version, which comes from Charles Perrault's 1697 fairytale *La Belle au Bois Dormant* ("The Beauty Asleep in the Woods"), and which Perrault adapted from a 1634 tale by Giambattista Basile, is hardly a love fantasy. It is a stark portrayal of the moral darkness that stems from lust and carnality. The kisser is not a prince, but a king, who violates the Sleeping Beauty, rather than reawaken her. Disney's version focuses on the idealistic-mythical side of love; the original one on the darker and more brutal side. Disney deals with fantasy, *agape*, and sacred love, Perrault with reality, *eros*, and profane carnality. The line between these domains is reflected in the stories we have always told about the love-sex opposition and its position on the continuum that involves the body, the spirit (mind), and the world (reality).

The sacred was mythologized in Greek culture as the realm of Apollo—the god of beauty and the fine arts—and the profane as the realm of Dionysus—the god of wine, representing the irrational, undisciplined, and orgiastic side of the psyche. Profane love stories are Dionysian, portraying all that is carnal and orgiastic; sacred ones (such as the love fantasies of medieval lore) are Apollonian encompassing all that is spiritual. This dualism is found in narrative traditions throughout the world. As the Jungian scholar Joseph L. Henderson aptly observes, the opposition takes on various symbolic and ritualistic forms[2]:

Some men need to be aroused, and experience their initiation in the violence of a Dionysiac "thunder rite." Others need to be subdued, and they are brought to submission in the ordered design of temple precinct or sacred cave, suggestive of the Apollonian religion of later Greece. A full initiation embraces both themes, as we can see when we look either at the material drawn from ancient texts or at living subjects.

We are emotionally drawn to stories that deal with love in both fantasy (*agape*) and realistic (*eros*) ways. Perhaps nowhere as in Romantic and Neo-Romantic opera has the dualism of love been portrayed as powerfully and memorably. This is perhaps why these operas remain staples of the repertoire to this very day. One of the most beloved of all such operas, *La Traviata* (The Wayward One), was composed by Giuseppe Verdi and first performed in 1853. Its libretto is based on the French drama, *La dame aux Camélias* (The Lady of the Camellias), by Alexandre Dumas. The plot takes place in and around Paris in the mid-1800s, recounting the tragic story of Violetta, the heroine, who leads an immoral life as an ailing courtesan until she falls unexpectedly in love with Alfredo, a handsome young nobleman, who declares his own desperate love for her in the first act. Wanting to avoid the power of love, she struggles with her indecision. In Act III, she sings the haunting aria, *Addio del passato*, in which she bids farewell to her past, surrendering ineluctably to love and thus agreeing reluctantly to a love affair with Alfredo, even though she is dying of consumption. The two lovers move in together to the countryside. One day while Alfredo is away his father, Giorgio Germont, visits her in order to plead with her to end the affair because of the scandal it is causing in high society. Violetta agrees to do so, even though she is heartbroken. She returns reluctantly to her previous life, and when Alfredo finds her at a party in the company of a former lover, he angrily berates her for her unfaithfulness, and before storming out he throws money in her face in repayment for her previous love, scorning her role as a courtesan. In the last stages of her illness, Germont visits Violetta and tells her that he revealed the truth of their breakup to Alfredo. Alfredo comes back to her, full of shame and remorse, hoping desperately to live together with her in happiness. But her health deserts her and she dies, as reality intervenes to shatter the fairytale ending tragically.

Another famous opera composed by Verdi, which plays powerfully on the psychic tension between the idealism and tragedy of love, and the nefarious ramifications of revenge, is *Il Trovatore* (The Troubadour), first performed in 1853, and based on the Spanish play *El Trovador* by Antonio García Gutiérrez. The plot takes place in 1400s Spain, in the midst of troubadour culture when, as discussed previously, the ideal of love was the motivating force of the poetry and music of the era. The story revolves around the troubadour Manrico, who falls madly in love with Leonora, a noblewoman. To complicate matters, the Count di Luna also loves Leonora. As fate would have it, the count and Manrico are brothers, although only the gypsy Azucena knows it. Azucena seeks revenge against the Count because his father had her own mother burned at the stake. The love affair between Manrico and Leonora is doomed by the repercussions of revengeful retribution. The jealous Count has Manrico executed so that he can have Leonora for himself, but she retreats to a nunnery where she eventually kills herself, preferring death to life without Manrico. After Manrico's death, Azucena reveals to the Count the fateful truth that he has killed his own brother, gaining the revenge she so fervently sought. The themes of obsession, revenge, violence, and murder seem to crop up frequently in love stories, from the tale of Medusa to *Il Trovatore* and beyond, suggesting that love is much more than a simple romantic feeling, but rather something that is intertwined with destiny, power, jealousy, and the mystery of human life—an amalgam of contrasting powerful emotions that constantly crop up in tales of love.

In the early twentieth century, Giacomo Puccini became the heir to Verdi's legacy, shaping his operas, however, with more realism. *Tosca*, first performed in 1900 and based on the French play *La Tosca* by Victorien Sardou, is one of Puccini's most well-known portrayals of the fantasy-realism dualism inherent in love affairs. The story takes place in 1800s Rome, an era of political intrigue. Floria Tosca, a famous singer, and Mario, a painter, are fervently and passionately in love. But the villainous scoundrel, Baron Scarpia, the chief of police, desires Tosca for himself. A political prisoner, Cesare Angelotti, has escaped from Scarpia. Tosca and Mario know his hiding place, and Scarpia attempts to force them to reveal where he is hiding, threatening to execute Mario if they do not reveal Angelotti's whereabouts. In the final scene, Scarpia attempts to violate Tosca, but she kills him and then commits suicide, after seeing a firing squad execute her beloved Mario. In Puccini, the love-leads-to-death formula, which is evocative of the medieval tales of Paolo and Francesca and Romeo and Juliet, takes a starkly realistic turn, with villainy and malevolence incapable of defeating love, even if the result is catastrophic.

A few years later, in 1905, the opera *Salome*, composed by Richard Strauss, and based on a play by Oscar Wilde, takes the dualism in an even more gruesome direction, with such violence and harshness that it shocked audiences at the time. Wilde based his play on the story of Salome in the New Testament, but he added details and made modifications that scandalized the audiences of his era. Strauss reflected the shocking content through the gut-wrenching music of his opera. The plot takes place in the palace of King Herod, around 30 CE. In the midst of a banquet, the religious prophet Saint John the Baptist is heard screaming the prophecy of the coming messiah from his prison cell. Salome, who is Herod's stepdaughter, is attracted passionately to Saint John who, however, repudiates her advances. So she decides to take revenge. Herod asks Salome to dance for him, promising her anything she wishes in return. Salome performs the famous "Dance of the Seven Veils" and then asks Herod for Saint John's head on a silver dish. Though horrified, Herod keeps his promise and has Saint John beheaded. In a gruesome scene, Salome kisses the head of the prophet. This may be one of the most ghastly of all crimes of passion recorded by history and fiction.

The same kind of stark realism is obvious in Alban Berg's 1925 opera *Wozzeck*, based on the play *Woyzeck* by Georg Büchner. The story is about Wozzeck, a soldier in the Austrian army around 1830. He is frequently abused and ridiculed by his superiors. And even worse, the woman he loves, Marie, deceives him with another man. Driven insane by jealousy, Wozzeck stabs and kills Marie, throwing the knife into a pond and, ironically, drowning while searching for it. The music is jarring, dissonantly capturing the contrasting emotions that love evokes. Berg followed this masterpiece with *Lulu*, based on two dramas by Frank Wedekind. Berg died in 1935, leaving the work unfinished. The incomplete opera received its first performance in 1937. Recalling the many femmes fatales of history, Lulu destroys her lovers one by one. The first victim is her elderly husband, who is killed after finding her in bed with a young painter. The latter marries Lulu, but after meeting a Doctor Schön, who tells him about Lulu's past, the painter commits suicide. Lulu seduces Schön to marry her, but she continues her sexual escapades with other men, including with Schön's own son Alwa. Lulu murders Schon after an argument, but this time she is arrested and found guilty. The Countess Geschwitz helps Lulu escape to London. There she lives as a prostitute with Alwa, the countess, and an elderly man named Schigolch. Sardonically, one of her clients turns out to be Jack the Ripper, who kills Lulu and then the countess. The tragic irony is palpable, leaving us with the sense that those who fall in love are fools, led on a leash by its unfathomable dark forces—when sex and the desire for power dominate, the result is death. Genuine love, if one is capable of it, provides a means of escaping this fate. Berg's opera shows what happens when love is absent.

Star-Crossed Lovers, Love Gods, and Love Goddesses

The image of two lovers alone, locked in a prolonged and tender kiss under the stars, is a prototypical one of ideal love. Star-crossed lover stories are ancient, as we have seen, although they gain momentum in the medieval ages. In the typical story, starlight passes through the two lovers to create an idyllic scene; but we know that their love is doomed from the start, because of the evil deeds of others or the devastating effects of going against the social grain.

To encode this scene indelibly into the imagination, Shakespeare was the one who coined the phrase "star-crossed lovers" in *Romeo and Juliet*, remaining a cliché ever since, both linguistically and culturally.

Star-crossed lovers—real and fictional—have been etched permanently into our imagination by their stories, transcending time: Orpheus and Eurydice, Samson and Delilah, Paolo and Francesca, Tristan and Isolde, Guinevere and Lancelot—and the list could go on and on. Perhaps our abiding interest in their stories is because they might contain the interpretive key to decoding the mystery of love within us. Stars are symbols of destiny and fate. The expression "star-crossed" is thus a perfect one, because it implies that the stars participate in the act of love, an act that will likely bring about consequences. Countless novels and movies continue to deal with this abiding theme. In them, love takes place at night, under the stars, otherwise it might lose is mystique, its power, becoming just the realization of a reproductive urge, leaving its disappointing traces in amorous relationships. Without romance, the promise of sex somehow seems to hold little meaning—ending up being just a form of biological release. But in that same act of star-crossed romance there is a fateful message that is always lurking below the threshold of awareness. The message is that it will not last and might even lead to a tragic end. As the late Italian actress, Anna Magnani, astutely put it, "Great passions, my dear, don't exist: they're liars' fantasies. What do exist are little loves that may last for a short or a longer while."[3] As these words imply, stories of star-crossed love are products of human fantasy. But while we may have to live with "little loves," we can certainly imagine loves that last forever, like the stars. Everlasting love is a fantasy, but it nonetheless motivates us to search for it in reality. The search itself is what is unconsciously meaningful and worthwhile.

The star-crossed love story became popular in the medieval period, defining its literature. It was an extension of the mythic narratives involving love goddesses and gods who ruled human destiny. The Bible too presents us with stories of personages with the capacity to affect human fate through the force of love and lust. For example, the personage of Lilith is a portrait of a femme fatale who commands love unto herself. According to one version of her story, God made Lilith out of earth. In paradise, she drew the amorous attention of Adam. But Lilith refused to submit to his passionate whims, deciding to flee from paradise. Upset, God sent three angels to bring her back, with the warning that if she refused to return, one of her children would die each day. Lilith was defiant, vowing to seek revenge herself if God took such action, by harming all newborn infants. Even more defiantly, she became a temptress, upsetting stable and staid human lives and challenging God's laws of fidelity in marriage. This is a story of love, vengeance, and power that pits human will against divine will. Lilith is a deeply-rooted archetype of defiance based in lust—a theme that appears in different guises in various tales throughout the world. In Western literature, Lilith appears notably in Goethe's *Faust* (1829) and in Bernard Shaw's *Back to Methuselah* (1922).

The legend of another Biblical personage, Jezebel, can also be listed under the same archetypal-narrative rubric. Jezebel, a Tyrian princess and daughter of Ethbaal, king of Tyre and Sidon, was given in marriage to Ahab, King of Israel. In one version of her story, she is condemned as bringing about the worship of Baal, the false idol and fertility god, through her sexual wiles and subterfuges, evoking repudiation from the authority figures of her era. But Jezebel always remained unfazed, coming across as a strong-willed, politically shrewd, and wholly insubordinate woman who dared to go against the moral laws of her era, with her irresistible seductive solicitations. Jezebel has been admired by writers ever since, from Shakespeare and Shelley to Joyce. Unlike common folk who must submit to such laws unthinkingly, Jezebel rises above them, like a goddess, ruling over men with her wit and sexual power.

The mythic tales of love gods also fall under this generic category. The classic example is the story of Adonis, the strikingly beautiful youth that young women could not resist. Aphrodite was particularly drawn to him. According to one version of the myth, Aphrodite left her husband to be with him. She warned Adonis of the dangers of hunting. But he did not heed her advice and was killed by Hephaestus, Aphrodite's jealous husband, disguised as a boar. According to another myth, Aphrodite placed the infant Adonis in a box as a gift to Persephone, a ruler of the underworld, for safekeeping. But Persephone became so enamored with the youth that she decided to keep him all for herself. To settle the quarrel between the goddesses, Zeus, decreed that Adonis would spend part of the year with Aphrodite and another part with Persephone. When Adonis was with Aphrodite on earth, vegetation flourished. When he was in the underworld, vegetation died. The Greeks used this myth to explain the change of the seasons, honoring Adonis in ceremonies and by cultivating plants that grew and died quickly. The story thus identifies love as an element in pathetic fallacy.

Love gods can also take on human form. The classic example is that of Don Juan, the legendary brigand hero and unrepentant libertine, whose story will be discussed again below. Don Juan makes women fall for him with his handsome looks, physical skills, and irresistible charms, and then always leaves them to pine over him and to run after him wherever he may be. As a moral scoundrel, Don Juan can only be punished by a higher power, since no human being can tame him. He is a dark love god who, although women know he is a rogue, still holds a strange emotional hold over them, with his promise of unending dangerous, but exciting, romance. The real-life Don Juan, and arguably the greatest lover of history, was the eighteenth century Italian adventurer and scoundrel Giacomo Casanova. He was irresistible to women to whom he turned his attention, at least according to legend. Casanova himself recounts his amorous exploits in his *Histoire de ma vie* (Story of My Life), in which he reveals that he had over 200 lovers, married, betrothed, and unmarried, enduring imprisonment and even death, to seduce them.[4]

The Don Juan-Casanova figure lives on in popular narratives, through movies, novels, and other media. The 1994 movie, *Don Juan De Marco*, even puts a sardonic and humorous twist to the legend. The story is about an older psychiatrist who attempts to help a patient who sees himself as the legendary Don Juan. Ironically, it is the psychiatrist himself who gains the most from their therapy sessions. The story starts with the patient believing that he is the great lover of folklore, donning a mask and cape. He is standing on top of a billboard, threatening to jump to his death. After being rescued, he is taken to a psychiatric facility where he is eventually placed under the supervision of the aging Dr. Jack Mickler, who is about to retire. The patient declares bluntly to Dr. Mickler that he is the great lover Don Juan. The reason, as we find out, is that he is suffering from a deep depression after being rebuffed by the woman of his dreams. As Mickler converses with the young man, who speaks ecstatically of the "art of love," the doctor himself realizes that the patient's description might actually help him revive his own failing amorous relationship with his wife, gradually becoming convinced that his patient might really be Don Juan. The subtext of the movie is that love is realizable if we can fantasize about it and then translate our fantasies into real life. We are all potentially great lovers, if we allow ourselves to imitate the lovers and the great love stories. They hold the real "therapy" for living a life ensconced in romance.

Star-crossed love existed in antiquity, of course, even though it was identified as such much later. The stories of Hero and Leander and Troilus and Cressida are cases-in-point. Hero was a stunningly gorgeous priestess of Aphrodite. She lived in a tower in Sestos, at the edge of the Hellespont, and Leander was a young handsome youth from Abydos on the other side of the strait. Leander fell desperately in love with Hero and would swim every night across the Hellespont to be with her in a loving embrace. Hero always lit a lamp at the top of her tower to help him find his way across the water. But, as in all star-crossed stories, the situation was doomed from the outset by some hidden quirk of destiny. During one stormy winter night, as Leander attempted to make his usual crossing, high waves tossed him into the sea as Hero's light was extinguished by the breezes. As a result, Leander drowned and, grief-stricken, Hero plunged to her death from the tower.

The story of Troilus and Cressida actually appeared in the twelfth century, becoming broadly known after Shakespeare turned it into a play much later. The story is set during the last years of the Trojan War. Troilus was the son of King Priam of Troy, and Cressida was the daughter of a Trojan soothsayer. They fall deeply in love, pledging eternal fidelity to each other. However, during the Trojan War, Cressida is taken prisoner and cannot resist the charms of Diomedes, a strong and handsome warrior. She betrays her beloved. Enraged and deeply hurt, Troilus plots his revenge, but ends up being the one who is killed. Can Cressida love both? Recalling the Calabrian folk song from the previous chapter, maybe love can be repeated over and over. But there always seem to be dreadful consequences in so doing, at least in our narratives.

No list of star-crossed lovers would be complete without the ill-fated love tryst between Antony and Cleopatra, which is part fiction, part history, and part star-crossed tale. Cleopatra had love affairs with both Julius Caesar and Mark Antony, both ceding instantly to her beauty, intelligence, and seductive wiles. Cleopatra became Caesar's mistress in Rome, going back to Egypt after he was assassinated in 44 BCE. Mark Antony then moved to Egypt to be with her, but as in many star-crossed love affairs, things do not work out and he returns to Rome to marry Octavia, a sister of Octavian who was heir to a part of Caesar's fortune. But his love of Cleopatra will not release him emotionally, and he goes back to be with her in 36 BCE. Furious, Octavian declares war against them. After the Battle of Actium in 31 BCE, the star-crossed lovers flee to Alexandria, where they both commit suicide, in true star-crossed lover fashion.

Cleopatra is a real-life love goddess, larger than life. In Act II, scene 2 of *Antony and Cleopatra*, Shakespeare describes her as follows:

Age cannot wither her, nor custom stale
Her infinite variety: other women cloy
The appetites they feed: but she makes hungry
Where most she satisfies.

The story of the historical love triangle between Cleopatra, Mark Antony, and Julius Caesar reads like a modern-day Harlequin romance story and has, in fact, inspired novels, movies, and TV programs. Stories of love, betrayal, and revenge seem to be inextricable from all other kinds of stories. We cannot seem to extricate love from any of our stories, real and fictional. One could easily write a supplementary history of humanity based on the famous stories of lovers and their trysts—a history that might reveal the true motivations behind many of our actions.

Dangerous Love

When one thinks of stories such as the Don Juan narrative, one hardly thinks of them as stories of romance. But a critical reading suggests that such narratives are indeed about love—more precisely, the dangerous side of love, forming an opposition with its purer side, as in the stories of star-crossed lovers. The subtext in the Don Juan narrative is about our bizarre fascination with the dark "dangerous lover" and the "dangerous liaisons" that such a lover gets people to engage in. The original Spanish tale comes from the Middle Ages. It is retold in theatrical form in *The Trickster of Seville* (1630), by Spanish playwright Tirso de Molina, in which a dark, handsome nobleman, named Don Juan Tenorio, seduces women who seem incapable of resisting his amorous overtures. When he is caught with the daughter of Don Gonzalo, the commander challenges him to a duel. Don Gonzalo is killed and Don Juan then visits his tomb, scornfully inviting the funerary statue of the commander to dinner, showing fearlessness and disdain for everything that is moral and even supernatural, seeing himself as above the law, human and divine. Surprisingly, the statue comes to life and accepts the invitation. The end for Don Juan comes when the statue takes his hand and drags him down into hell for his crimes against God and humankind. The story has intrigued writers and musicians ever since, including Mozart with his operatic masterpiece, *Don Giovanni* (1787). Why do the women in the legend fall for this scoundrel? The reason may well be that he brought a sense of danger and excitement to the love affair, allowing love to be enacted outside of its habitual and boring consummation in marriage and courtship.

Don Juan is a "Dracula figure," an archetype of a dangerous lover who comes out at night to upset the social status quo by kindling the erotic instinct as separate from romance, thus dismantling *eros* from *agape*, sexual intimacy from romance, the profane from the sacred. As is well known, the modern version of the Dracula narrative starts with Bram Stoker's novel of 1897. Coming at the end of the Romantic period, the figure of Dracula fit in perfectly with the times, challenging authority, exuding passion and sexual power, and resuscitating the mythic search for immortality. Belief in vampirism goes back to ancient times. But it came to the social surface in the eighteenth century when vampires were thought to be real creatures. The only way to render a vampire permanently dead—it was believed—was to drive a stake through his heart. Incidentally, Stoker had his vampire come out in daylight, but he became dangerous only at night, under the cloak of secrecy that night-time provides.

Since Stoker's novel, Hollywood has transformed Dracula into a suave nobleman, who is attractive and fascinatingly dangerous. His neck bite is highly erotic. Like the legendary Don Juan, Count Dracula is, arguably, the unconscious sublimation of a fantasy figure—a secret erotic lover whose attraction is the dangerous liaisons he promises to bring about. Dracula ravishes his sexual prey, whereupon they are transformed into vampires themselves. The vampire story may be the first one in the genre of "dark erotic literature," as it can be called. Goethe and Coleridge even created stories about female vampires in *The Bride of Corinth* (1797) and *Christabel* (1800) respectively. In 1872, Sheridan Lefau describes a lesbian vampire in his novel *Camilla*—a novel that inspired Roger Vadim's *Mourir de Plaisir* (1962). The vampire story is, of course, related in spirit to Gothic literature, which starts with Horace Walpole's, *The Castle of Otranto* (1764). The Gothic tale revolves around romance as unfolding late at night, in dark places (such as castles), and involving dangerous lovers and the liaisons they spawn. The Gothic romance continues today in popular novels, movies, and programs that turn the star-crossed lover story on its head—it also takes place at night, but not under the stars, and rather than inspire fondness and affection, it incites fear, dread, and erotic energy. The Gothic novel is an irresistible blend of horror and romance, love and fear. The style inspired the novels of the Brontë sisters, and American writers like Nathaniel Hawthorne, Herman Melville, and Edgar Allan Poe.

The erotic subtext in the Dracula myth was brought out in clever fashion by the 1979 remake of *Nosferatu* (1922), the first Dracula film, titled *Nosferatu the Vampyre*, and directed by Werner Herzog. The tortured, bald, fanged and pointy-eared Dracula attempts to sexually possess Lucy Harker. He follows her to her room, preceded by his ominous distorted shadow. To her wide-eyed reflection in the mirror he bellows in a dark seductive tone: "You must excuse my rude entrance. I am Count Dracula. Come to me and be my ally. The absence of love is the most abject pain." Being sexually pure, she declines the offer. It is only later that, in true sacrificial style, she offers herself up to him, wearing a white gown. During that scene, we see her lying perfectly still as she awaits his kiss, but he starts by groping her with his long-fingered hand. Then he slowly descends to bite her neck and feed upon her. The eroticism is tangible, as is its inherent danger. But, in typical ironic Herzog fashion, it is all a ploy to keep Dracula in an erotic trance until the rays of the new sun come in through the window, sealing his fate.

Overall, such stories are portrayals of the "dark side" of love, juxtaposing the idyllic "love-under-the-stars" scene with a "love-in-the-dark" one. Adding fear to the chemistry of love seems to heighten our experience of romance by adding a thrilling element to it. Romance thus takes on a feral, undomesticated, and untamable turn, projecting us into a "danse macabre" of the heart. A passionate kiss exchanged in a Gothic castle, in a dark alley, or anywhere else under the cloak of night is tinged with a blend of eroticism and terror, producing a "haunting" thrill. Gothic stories, the Don Juan legend, and all kinds of dangerous love stories simultaneously evoke the emotions of fear and love, suggesting that the two are indeed inextricably intertwined. The Gothic romance novel flew initially in the face of traditions, confronting them by packing the two emotions—*eros* and *agape*—into one narrative formula. In addition to star-crossed lovers and the usual cast of evil villains, Gothic romances include ghostly and supernatural beings such as magicians, vampires, werewolves, monsters, demons, perambulating skeletons, and the like.

Novelist Ann Radcliffe, a leading exponent of the Gothic novel, conveys the angst we feel from the emotional tug within us between the two love forces (*eros* and *agape*), through the figure of the dark brooding lover, who, like Don Juan, is irresistible and will upset the emotional applecart irrevocably. Her best known work is the four-volume, *Mysteries of Udolpho* (1794), which inspired imitations and adaptations, such as the *roman noir* ("black novel") in France and the *Schauerroman* ("shudder novel") in Germany. Radcliffe herself became cross-influenced by these new trends.

The Gothic genre (and its derivatives) produced its own cast of Gothic star-crossed lovers, such as Quasimodo and Esmeralda, in Victor Hugo's, *The Hunchback of Notre Dame* (1831) and Heathcliffe and Catherine, in Emily Brontë's *Wuthering Heights* (1847). Hugo's masterpiece takes place during 1400s Paris, centering on Quasimodo, a hunchbacked and deformed bell ringer who lives in the Notre Dame Cathedral, hiding from people and their the derisive chants. At one point, a struggling poet named Pierre Gringoire encounters a beautiful gypsy woman and street dancer, Esmeralda. After dancing seductively, he follows her home. He sees her being attacked by Quasimodo and a monk named Frollo, who lusts for her. Gringoire rushes to help her but is knocked out by Quasimodo, who is about to kill him when the king's Archers arrive in time and capture the hunchback. But Gringoire is not off the hook. A group of thieves are about to hang him in place of Quasimodo. Gringoire is saved by Esmeralda when she promises to marry him. Quasimodo is put on trial and sentenced to torture exposed to the humiliating chants of a rabble crowd, who hate him for his deformity. He begs for water, and it is the kind-hearted Esmeralda who eventually brings him something to drink. To make a long story short, at first, Esmeralda finds it repulsive to look at Quasimodo, but they form a friendship, and she takes up a temporary home in the Notre Dame cathedral, with Quasimodo who falls madly in love with her, looking after her with great care. Esmeralda is eventually ordered to be removed from Notre Dame. But when Quasimodo sees people come to the cathedral, he believes that they have come to kill her. So he defends her, killing a large number of the intruders. The opportunist Frollo used the commotion as a diversion to sneak Esmeralda out of the cathedral, offering two choices: admit that she loves him or be executed. She chooses the latter. From the top of a tower in the cathedral, Quasimodo sees Esmeralda in a white dress hanging from the executioner's scaffold. He screams out in despair, grabbing Frollo by the neck and throwing him from the tower to his death. Quasimodo is never seen again. Years later a gravedigger stumbles across Esmeralda's remains. In her tomb he finds the skeleton of a hunchback curled around her.

This is a Gothic story of the power of love to change one's life, no matter the disfigurement of the body. The story is dark and dangerous in another sense—it tells how love can become an obsession, leading to tragedy and death. Its force is inevitable, no matter who is involved—a handsome Don Juan, a dark sinister vampire, or a hunchback.

In Emily Brontë's masterpiece, the story revolves around Heathcliff's love for Catherine Earnshaw, the woman with whom he had been raised as an orphan boy. It takes place, in typical Gothic style, in an ominous place called Wuthering Heights. Heathcliff falls deeply and irrevocably in love with Catherine. But overhearing that a marriage between the two would be degrading and thus impossible, Heathcliff flees the home and Catherine subsequently marries the wealthy Edgar Linton. After becoming rich himself, the enraged and heartbroken Heathcliff decides to go back to Wuthering Heights, whereupon he elopes with Linton's sister, in a scheme to punish Catherine and gain revenge on Linton. When Catherine dies in childbirth, Heathcliff becomes forsaken and desperate, bearing a sense of guilt for the rest of his life. The novel was condemned when it was first published for its lack of conventional morality, and its glorification of dark passion.

Don Juan, Quasimodo, and Heathcliff are dark figures in the love narrative. In the case of Quasimodo, his overwhelming love for Esmeralda turns him into a pathetic yet endearing figure. Heathcliff is also pathetic, but less worthy of endearment because of his vengeful plan. Don Juan exudes danger, like the Dracula figure, and thus evokes within us a sense of the danger of erotic love. They exemplify what Carl Jung called the Shadow archetype—emanating from the "dark side" of the psyche.[5] Characters like Heathcliff and the others bring the dark side out into the open, where it can be examined and tamed; its repression, on the other hand, might have unwanted consequences. As Jung observed: "Everyone carries a shadow and the less it is embodied in the individual's conscious life, the blacker and denser it is."[6] Jung also believed that: "In spite of its function as a reservoir for human darkness—or perhaps because of this—the Shadow is the seat of creativity."[7] This might explain our fascination with dark lovers and dangerous liaisons. Like the ancient and medieval myths of demons and monsters, the dangerous lover narrative is a projection of the Shadow that allows us, perhaps, to eliminate our own shadows, examining them in the form of narrative where they can be rendered harmless. The dangerous lover is a Shadow figure who is felt as a threat to the wellbeing of society, atrophying us into believing that unbridled sexual energy is part of an emotional imperative. He is a monster who takes human form.

One of the best-known portrayals of the monster in Gothic literature is *Frankenstein* (1818) by Mary Shelley, which tells the story of Victor Frankenstein, a scientist who tries to create a living being for the good of humanity but instead produces a monster. He creates his creature by assembling parts of dead bodies and then activating the creature with electricity. The monster is actually gentle and intelligent. But everyone fears and mistreats him, like Quasimodo, because of his hideous appearance. Frankenstein himself rejects him, refusing to make a mate for him. The monster's terrible loneliness drives him to seek revenge by murdering his creator's wife, brother, and best friend. There is an ominous subtext here—the lack of love may turn someone into a murderer. Subsequent Gothic novels such as *Ormond* (1799), *The Partisan* (1835), and *The Monks of Monk Hall* (1845) all "present multiple body counts and Shadow villains in which one can see the literary prototypes of the contemporary American serial murderer," as Philip Simpson remarks.[8]

Stories of murder provoked by the desire to be loved or by the need to control others emotionally abound. In ancient China, for example, it is said that the Prince of Jidong murdered at least 100 people to assert himself as the most desirable of all aristocrats.[9] The Hungarian noblewoman, Elizabeth Báthory, killed over 650 young women in the early 1600s, recalling the evil queens of fairytales.[10] She was labeled a vampire, an epithet that was likely assigned to her as a means of coping psychologically and socially with the brutal deaths. Báthory murdered only peasant and servant girls until 1609, allowing her to go undetected, or at least unpunished, for a long span of time, given that the families could not press charges against a noblewoman, especially one belonging to the richest family in Hungary, and to whom the King owed massive amounts of money. The torture of peasants and servants for minor offences or indiscretions was common at the time. It is said that Báthory witnessed her father torturing a servant by sewing him alive inside a dying horse, and her fiancé publicly castrated a servant with whom Bathóry had an affair, throwing him to a pack of wild dogs.[11] Such gruesome actions were considered to be socially acceptable responses to infidelity. It was only when Bathóry started killing upper class girls that she was finally prosecuted, bringing out the double standard based on class of her era. She started her murder spree after opening a finishing school, admitting 25 girls, and killing all of them, claiming falsely that some of the girls had killed the others due to jealousy over jewelry, and then committing suicide. The King sent his Palatine to investigate Bathóry. Several of Bathóry's accomplices were sentenced to death for their parts in the crimes, including a young boy, but Bathóry herself could not be executed, because of her position; she was sentenced to imprisonment in her castle for the rest of her life.

Another infamous female serial killer of pre-modern times, who seemingly killed for vampiristic and other dysfunctional sexual-narcissistic reasons, was Catherine Monvoison, a major figure in Louis XIV's seventeenth-century court. She provided poisons to those who wanted to kill their spouses or wealthy relatives. She also slit the throats of babies, so that they could be "used as living sacrifices at black masses, and their blood was used in a variety of witchcraft ceremonies."[12] She had access to the babies by providing a home for women with difficult pregnancies. Unlike Bathóry, Monvoison seems to have crafted her own image as a witch, and was almost convicted of witchcraft by the Church early in her career, but she was acquitted, leading to a widespread perception that her actions were sanctioned by the Church. Her husband was an unsuccessful jeweler, and she was forced to support her family, so she claimed, in her nefarious way.

In most of these dark stories the killing is traced to some inner urge for sexual power and control that is repressed by social mores, thus foreshadowing modern-day psychological theories of the psyche, such as the early one by psychiatrist Richard von Krafft-Ebing who, in his 1886 book *Psychopathia Sexualis*, describes the case of a French serial killer in the 1870s, named Eusebius Pieydagnelle, who murdered six people in order to drink their blood.[13] It seems that the vampire narrative itself had affected the murderer, spurring him on to commit his crimes. In an 1891 essay, "The Decay of Lying," presented in the form of a Socratic dialogue, Oscar Wilde stated that "Life imitates Art far more than Art imitates Life," challenging the long-standing Aristotelian notion of mimesis or the theory that art is an imitation of life.[14] Wilde turned it on its head because, as he put it, "the self-conscious aim of Life is to find expression."[15] Cases of real-life murderous love stories, enacting an inner urge to express the dark feelings generated by sexual urges, may actually corroborate Wilde's view, since they are, indirectly, evidence of how emotionally powerful the love instinct is in both its carnal and emotional facets. Wilde used the example of the London fog to make his case. Although fog has always existed in London, one notices the qualities and aesthetics of the fog because "poets and painters have taught the loveliness of such effects. They did not exist till Art had invented them."[16]

Some literary historians believe that ancient drama may have developed from the rituals performed by the secret mystery cults of ancient Greece, in which Pythagoras, Plato and other philosophers are said to have taken part.[17] The central purpose of those rituals appears to have been to pose questions about the nature of existence and to contemplate mysteries such as love and its power over human beings.[18] In an analogous way, we feel today that by solving crime mysteries that involve love, we may be decoding the mystery of love itself. It is thus little wonder that mystery stories invariably involve love and are among the most popular of all narrative genres.[19]

The Don Juan and Dracula figures exude passion and sexual power, resuscitating the mythic search for immortality. The potent combination of eroticism, fear, blood, and death, sends down many skeins of recognition into the unconscious mind. In the 1600s and 1700s vampire scares were reported in many parts of Europe. Buried corpses suspected of being vampires were dug up and staked through the heart. The first extended prose vampire story was The *Vampyre* (1819), by John Polidori. Starting with *Nosferatu*, the 1922 silent film directed by F. W. Murnau, loosely based on Stoker's novel, vampirism has been a staple of movie fare ever since. It can also be seen on television screens with programs (current and defunct) such as *Dark Shadows* (1969–1971), *Forever Knight* (1992–1996), *Buffy the Vampire Slayer* (1997–2003), *Blade* (2006–2007), among many others. Anne Rice's 1976 *Interview with the Vampire* is a perfect example of how the vampire myth has morphed into a modern-day love story, blending romance with dark sexuality. The novel was partly inspired by the death of her daughter from leukemia at the age of 5. Rice also wrote the screenplay for the successful 1994 motion-picture adaptation of the work. She is probably responsible for the trend today of equating adolescence psychologically with vampirism, with adolescence being a "dark stage," that is both a blessing and a curse. Rice's vampires are strangely vulnerable, lost in searching for true love.

Why are we so fascinated by the stories of dangerous lovers and dangerous liaisons? The potent combination of eroticism and danger seems to send shivers up and down our spine, awakening hidden desires. The dangerous lover challenges authority, symbolizing, perhaps, our desperate search for eternal youth, love, and immortality. The dark love story turns the star-crossed one upside down, and it includes stories of love monsters, such as werewolves. According to legend, the werewolf is a nocturnal beast, half human, half wolf, who seeks to satisfy his desires by hunting down victims, like real wolves. The figure comes originally from the Greek myth of Lycaon, a wicked ruler who aimed to murder Zeus. Failing to do so, Zeus turned him into a werewolf. In some werewolf stories, the forlorn lover transforms himself into a wolf by donning a wolf skin, drinking water from a puddle left by a wolf's footprint, or by rubbing a magic ointment on his body. In other stories, the man is transformed into a wolf through a magic spell. The best known story of this kind is *Little Red Riding Hood*, whose origins are traced back to a tenth-century folktale in Italy, and inscribed into the fairytale literature by both Charles Perrault and the Brothers Grimm. In the original version, the little girl does not survive the wolf attack. She does, of course, in milder versions. Interestingly, ever since that tale, a rapacious man is called a "wolf." The people in the stories who are threatened by werewolves use various methods to bring them back to human form. These methods include saying the werewolf's real name, hitting the werewolf three times on the forehead, or making the sign of the cross.

Epilogue

Stories of romance start in antiquity and continue to be everywhere in modernity. We are attracted to them, arguably, because we need to decode the meaning of love and why it overwhelms us and guides our life choices. Stories in which people have given up fame and fortune for love are numerous. Love is an unstoppable force, inducing us to give up everything to follow its archer. The imagination has never been so imaginative than when it applies itself to writing about love and romance.

But whatever the historical period, the romance story and its subgenres depict the same kinds of themes and archetypes everywhere, no matter the language or culture. As a distinct genre, the love story started to proliferate around the 1100s, gaining wide popularity. The stories were called romances, not only because they dealt with knightly combat, adventure, intrigue, courtship, and love, legitimate or otherwise, but also because they were written in the languages of the people, rather than in Latin (the official language of writing). The legends and stories about King Arthur and the Knights of the Round Table were among the most popular of these, remaining so in different adaptations to this day. They have left their residues in today's popular culture, where chivalric themes crop up constantly. So too have the stories of dangerous love, which find their way into narratives of love affairs, betrayal, and crimes of passion. There may be modern-day twists and turns to the plot and to the outcome, but the romantic ingredients do not vary very much. Needless to say, the stories may be unrealistic and misleading. But they are enjoyable because they allow us to dream about love as an ideal. The characters may live exciting lives, but they seem always to end up with an emotional scar or some other price to pay. But it is a price that we are willing to pay for the promise of true and everlasting love.

The fairytale ending is something we all crave, whether we admit it or not. But it rarely happens. Even the famous stories of star-crossed lovers were always denied this ending. The kiss under the stars was fleeting, not everlasting. Only in fairytales does the kiss bring about a "happily ever after" result. Maybe we all want a fairytale ending to our romantic adventures and, if we can get it only in stories, so be it. This brings us to one of the most powerful love stories of modernity—the 1988 movie *(Nuovo) Cinema Paradiso.* The story starts with a scene in which we see a village priest acting as movie censor, demanding that kissing scenes to be cut out from films. Much of what was removed would not cause the slightest stir today even in younger audiences. Kissing closes out the film when the grown up character in the movie, Totò, views a reel of film that Alfredo, the movie projectionist, mentor, and ersatz father, left for him before he died. The reel is a collage of all the footage that the priest had asked Alfredo to take out. It brings tears to Totò's eyes. The reel also contained a shot of Totò and Elena kissing, which he did not know existed. Totò and Elena were star-crossed lovers, losing contact with each other through simple happenstance. At that point the film reel ends, as does the movie (Fig. 4.1).

Whether it is a fairytale, a story about star-crossed lovers, a Gothic novel, a tale about love scoundrels, or vampiristic lovers, the love narrative provides evidence that we are fascinated by the phenomenon of love and its ability to alter and drive human history. Narrative is an instinctual capacity, as can be seen from the fact that from the beginning of life we respond to stories intuitively, with no tutoring as to what they are. Indeed, they come so natural to us that they constitute both how we come to know the world culturally (through founding myths) and personally (through the childhood stories to which we are exposed in cultural context). One of the oldest story formats of all is about love and what it tells us about the human condition.

Fig. 4.1   *Cinema Paradiso Poster* (1983) (Wikimedia Commons)

Notes

1. Janice Radway, *Reading the Romance: Women, Patriarchy, and Popular Literature* (London, Verso, 1991).
2. Joseph L. Henderson, "Ancient Myths and Modern Man," in Carl G. Jung (ed.), *Man and His Symbols*, (New York: Dell, 1964), p. 146.
3. The quotation by Anna Magnani is taken from Oriana Fallaci's, *The Egotists* (New York: H. Regnery, 1963).
4. Giacomo Casanova, *The Story of My Life* (Harmondsworth: Penguin, 2001).
5. Carl Jung, *The Portable Jung* (Harmondsworth: Penguin, 1971).

6. Ibid., p. 12.
7. Ibid., p. 12.
8. Philip Simpson, *Psycho Paths: Tracking the Serial Killer Through Contemporary American Film and Fiction* (Chicago: Southern Illinois University Press 2000), p. 31.
9. Sima Qian, *Han Dynasty: Records of the Grand Historian I* (New York: Columba University Press, 1993).
10. Peter Vronsky, *Serial Killers: The Method and Madness of Monsters* (New York: Berkley. 2007), p. 78.
11. Tony Thorne, *Countess Dracula: The Life and Times of the Blood Countess, Elisabeth Báthory* (London: Bloomsbury, 1997), p. 3.
12. Dirk C. Gibson, *Legends, Monsters, or Serial Murderers? The Real Story Behind an Ancient Crime* (Santa Barbara: Praeger, 2012), p. 73.
13. Richard von Krafft-Ebing, *Psychopathia Sexualis* (Stuttgart: Ferdinand Enke, 1886).
14. Oscar Wilde, *Complete Works*, ed. by Josephine M. Guy, volume 4 (Oxford: Oxford University Press, 2007), p. 94.
15. Ibid., p. 94.
16. Ibid., p. 95.
17. Jeffrey Mishlove, *The Roots of Consciousness* (New York: Marlowe & Company, 1993), p. 40.
18. Many P. Hall, *The Secret Teachings of All Ages* (Los Angeles: Philosophical Research Society, 1973).
19. Marcel Danesi, *The Puzzle Instinct: The Meaning of Puzzles in Human Life* (Bloomington: Indiana University Press, 2002).

5

Love Images

Art and love are the same thing: It's the process of seeing yourself in things that are not you.
—Chuck Klosterman (b. 1972)

Prologue

If there is one work of visual art that can be interpreted as epitomizing the unity of body and soul in romantic love, it is Rodin's marvelous 1886 sculpture, the *Kiss*, which shows the nude figures of the star-crossed lovers of medieval lore, Paolo and Francesca, in a passionate yet tender embrace (Chap. 1). Rodin described it as "complete in itself and artificially set apart from the surrounding world."[1] Although it was originally intended to be part of the *Gates of Hell*, a bronze portal commissioned for a planned museum of art in Paris in 1889, Rodin did not feel that the image of the two lovers in an intimate embrace fit into the theme of the portal, even though Dante had put them in a circle of hell in his *Divine Comedy*. So, he decided to turn his sculpture into a freestanding work. It now defines what love "looks like" to virtually anyone who views it. The nude lovers are joined to each other, body and soul, in an act of intimacy and vulnerability at once. A bronze version of the sculpture (74 centimeters high) was sent for display to the 1893 World's Columbian Exposition in Chicago. At the time, it was deemed obscene and thus unsuitable for general viewing, relegated to an inner chamber with admission to adults only. The inability to distinguish the body-in-love from the body-in-lust

© The Author(s) 2019
M. Danesi, *The Semiotics of Love*, Semiotics and Popular Culture,
https://doi.org/10.1007/978-3-030-18111-6_5

has always been problematic in the interpretation of artistic representations of love and romance.

Sculptures, paintings, and photographs constitute yet another source for semiotically deciphering the meanings of love. To use a cliché, in this case seeing is truly believing. The words, metaphors, and phrases people have coined to encode the various feelings associated with the love-sex opposition provide mental forms for thinking about them (Chap. 3); the stories told and written about lovers, romances, pure and dark, including myths and fairytales, inform us about how we have connected love to history, how we understand relationships in narrative ways, and so on (Chap. 4); the visual images and scenes created by artists literally "show" us what love is about (present chapter). The third-century philosopher Plotinus claimed that art revealed the true nature of an object more accurately than just viewing it with the eyes, raising our experience of the mundane to a contemplation of universal truths. The most precious moments of life are those aesthetic instants when the soul is united, through art, with the divine.

Of all the grand visions conjured up by the human imagination, few captivate us more than the moment when lovers lock in an intimate embrace or a passionate kiss, as in the Rodin sculpture. The painters and sculptors who have made love the object of their imaginations are among the greatest of all time. They include Titian, Rubens, Canova, Munch, Schiele, Chagall, Matisse, Toulouse-Lautrec, Rodin, and Hayez, to mention but a handful. They have left us a powerful "pictography" of love that speaks to our eyes and heart directly.[2]

Art for Love's Sake

The capacity to draw and extract meaning from pictures is a truly extraordinary endowment of human evolution. There seems to be an "art instinct" within us that allows people, regardless of age, class, or talents, to represent a complex range of feelings and emotions in visual forms and media. Like language and narratives, artistic works and traditions are passed on from generation to generation throughout the world, in an effort to preserve precious visual documents that have great value for understanding ourselves. Defining art, however, is as impossible to do as defining love. Art is something that everyone recognizes intuitively, but which no one can quite define. All that can be said is that, starting in prehistory, drawing has allowed humans to represent their feelings and thoughts through images. From the ancient sculptures of anonymous artists that adorned the public square, to the abstract expressionist works of modernity, art presents us with a unique opportunity to examine the history of love as portrayed by the imaginations of artists.

Art works in public settings indicate that art has always had a social function. The notion of artists as eccentric creators is a relatively modern one, starting in the Romantic period. In ancient cultures, art was used as part of communal ceremonies. It was made by members of the community with artistic abilities, rather than by professional artists. In traditional aboriginal cultures of North America art continues, in fact, to be perceived as one aspect of community rituals that are designed to ensure a good harvest or to celebrate a significant life event such as a birth or a marriage. But even in modern urban cultures, art entails social meanings. Hanging a painting in an art gallery invites an individualistic appreciation; while drawing something on a city wall, such as graffiti, invites social reprobation or participation.

The first aesthetic theory of any scope was that of Plato, who believed that art was an attempt to represent in material form images that already exist in the mind. So, the sculptor takes a clump of marble and gives it the form of a human body that existed in the imagination. However, in the sculpture we discover many more things about the body than by simply viewing real bodies in the world—the representation of the artist is ideal, giving a particular shape and form to the real. The hidden truth about the body is in the clump; but it takes the artist to discover it. Plato also felt that art encouraged immorality, and that certain art works caused laziness and immoderacy. He wanted to banish some types of artists from his ideal republic. Aristotle also saw art as representation, but not in the same way that his teacher Plato did. The role of art, thought Aristotle, was to complete what nature did not finish, separating form from its physical manifestations, such as the imagined human body from its appearance as various shapes in people, and then transferring that form onto some artistic medium, such as canvas or marble. Thus, art was not imitation of the ideal, but rather a particular modeling of things that had the capacity to affect observers and thus transform their worldview—literally a different way of seeing things. Art in the Middle Ages functioned above all else as a visual language; that is, given that most people were illiterate, the paintings and sculptures that were created for churches and other religious locations spoke to the believers visually. The themes of this visual language were episodes in Christianity such as the Nativity, the Crucifixion, the Assumption, etc. It was during the Renaissance that art acquired more secular functions. That period, moreover, saw little difference between the artist and the scientist. Indeed, many were both—Leonardo da Vinci was a painter, writer, and scientist, Michelangelo a visual artist and poet. The view of the artist as a unique kind of genius impelled by creative impulses, free from the shackles of the routines of everyday humdrum, is very much a product of Romanticism, as mentioned; that was the period in which "art for art's sake" crystallized as a cultural leitmotif. In ancient times artists were laborers, paid by rulers for their services. In Ancient Egypt they were hired to build structures designed to glorify the pharaoh and life after death. Artists, like other trades people, customarily followed the family profession. It was only after the eighteenth century that the choice to become an artist was dictated mainly by personal choice, not by family tradition.

One of the most common artistic themes of antiquity was the spiritual nature of love—a kind of "art for love's sake" leitmotif. A classic example is the anonymous ancient Greek statue known as the Venus de Milo, which actually represents Aphrodite, (Chap. 2). Even if bare-breasted, the statue encapsulates the spiritual beauty and presence that Aphrodite possessed, rather than any sexual innuendo; her ethereal expression bespeaks of other-worldliness, as befitting her divinity. But, even in antiquity, the other artistic side if *agape* is *eros*, which is the motif behind many other ancient sculptures such as those of Bacchus, the god of wine, and of his acolytes, the satyrs. The latter are portrayed as lustful, drunken creatures of the forest with horse ears, tails, and horns. They

Fig. 5.1 *Two Satyrs and a Nymph Cortege (Attica, second century BCE)* (Wikimedia Commons)

bespeak of the mischievous erotic side of love. Aphrodite's sculpture is an idealization of *agape*; the sculptures of the satyrs a portrayal of *eros*. The contrast is striking and compelling. Above is a reproduction of an ancient relief (second century BCE) of two satyrs with a cortege of nymphs above them (Fig. 5.1):

Why is such art so effective emotionally, no matter who produces it or at which period of time it was produced? Perhaps the best-known, and most widely-accepted, theory for explaining the potency of art is the one put forward by the American philosopher Susanne Langer during the middle part of the twentieth century.[3] We do not experience art, she emphasized, as individual bits and pieces (shapes, tints, etc.), but as a holistic experience. It is only when individuals try to understand rationally why the art work had such an effect on them that the holistic experience is transformed by reasoning and language into one in which its parts can be taken apart, discussed, critiqued, and so on, like the individual words in a sentence. But, no matter how many times people try to understand the aesthetic experience discursively, it somehow escapes complete rational understanding, remaining larger than the sum of its parts. One can analyze the statue of Aphrodite as a combination of feminine physical features, a beautiful and divine face, etc. But these come into focus as components of the work only when we wish to consider them separately. When we see the statue initially, we hardly focus on these bits and pieces, but on the overall meaning of the work.

Art for love's sake has existed since prehistoric times, as briefly mentioned. The cave art going back some 30,000 years includes vivid images of people embracing each other or in other poses that suggest both love and fertility. The small sculptures of female figures found at archeological sites appear to blend the two sides of love in the same image. Since our origins, we have been fascinated by the love-sex conundrum that seems to beset our consciousness, translating it into images where it can be contemplated, as Langer so aptly put it. As Roland Barthes pointed out in 1964, visual images reveal how we think and what is of great importance to us.[4] From the beginning of time, it is obvious that love figures prominently in the imagination of those who have the talent to draw and sculpt skilfully.

An acclaimed critical study of visual representation is the one by John Berger, titled *Ways of Seeing*.[5] Berger actually wrote his book in a hybrid script to materially illustrate his thesis—in four of the chapters he used a combination of words and images, and in the remaining three only images. Berger's work shows practically that we read images and words in a hybrid fashion. Rudolph Arnheim's classic book, *Visual Thinking*,[6] also showed how pictures are powerful signs for interpreting our world, challenging the traditional differentiation in psychology between "thinking" versus "perceiving." He disputed the premise that verbal language comes before perception and that words are the triggers of thought. For Arnheim, perception and visual expression are what allow us to have a true understanding of our experiences of the world. Extending both Berger's and Arnheim's approaches, it is obvious that those art works that have been created to represent love since antiquity have brought to consciousness our intuitive perception of what love means to us. Arnheim claimed that we are naturally inclined to use visual thinking in order to come to grips with questions about life, because these can be more easily envisaged in images, rather than words. Art thus complements metaphor and poetry in producing insights into the phenomenon of love. It is a manifestation of the creative faculty that the Italian philosopher Vico called *fantasia* (Chap. 3).[7]

For Vico, the *fantasia* is the universal capacity to think imaginatively—literally, the ability to create mental images of experiences, feelings, perceptions, etc. It is the basis of metaphor, poetry, and art. The organization of all cultures is universally imaginative, based upon, and guided by, conscious bodily experiences that have been transformed into generalized forms by the *fantasia*. The *fantasia* thus liberates human beings from the constraints imposed on all other organisms by biology. As Donald Verene has aptly put it, the *fantasia* allows humans "to know from the inside" by extending "what is made to appear from sensation beyond the unit of its appearance and to have it enter into connection with all else that is made by the mind from sensation."[8] Love can only be understood through the *fantasia* and its metaphorical, poetic, and artistic expressions. These provide access to its *raison d'être*, more so than any scientific theory, as claimed several times in this book.

In support of Arnheim's idea that visuality is more fundamental cognitively than verbal cognition, it should be observed that historically there is no discontinuity between pictography and alphabets—the latter is a derivative of the former. In Phoenician, the word *beth* meant "house." Now, the Phoenicians took the first sound of that word, "B," as the picture word for "house." After a while, they came to use the same symbol to stand for the same sound wherever it occurred in other words. So, the shape of a letter was at first the simplified design of something whose name began with the sound that the letter represents. This new form of compressed pictographic writing became common in the marketplaces of the Mediterranean area because it made the recording and reproduction of transactions rapid and efficient. Every alphabet character is the symbolic residue of a stylistic alteration to some earlier pictograph, thus anecdotally supporting Arnheim's theory that visual thinking precedes all other kinds of cognition.

Images of Idyllic Love

As a story of idyllic and fateful love, the Paolo and Francesca tale has inspired many artists, in addition to Rodin. Jean Auguste Dominique Ingres' 1819 painting of the two star-crossed lovers dramatizes the transformative power of their furtive passionate kiss and the foreboding destiny it harbors within it. The painting captures the moment when the two lovers kiss, as Gianciotto hides from their view, catching them in the act. The dual meaning of unfettered romantic love—a blend of passion and defiance—is brought out visually in this marvelous painting. Paolo is clearly the initiator, leaning his body into Francesca as she angles her face away from him. It is interesting to note that Paolo ends up kissing her on the neck, not the lips, as the legend traditionally has it, adding a tinge of subtle eroticism to the act. Nefariously and threateningly, Gianciotto stands, rapier drawn, in the dark background to the side. The contrast is stunning and stark, as Gianciotto's jealousy-driven vendetta is about to take place. Unlike the Rodin sculpture, which focuses on the power of love itself to unite two bodies, Ingres' painting emphasizes the sinister consequences that love may bring about (Fig. 5.2):

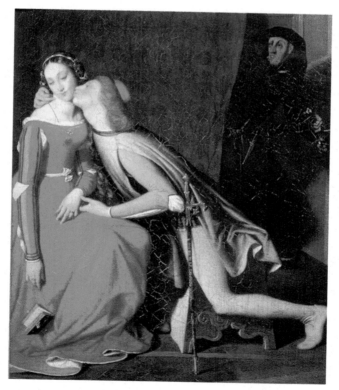

Fig. 5.2 *Paolo and Francesca (Jean Auguste Dominique Ingres, 1819)* (Wikimedia Commons)

In effect, the story of Paolo and Francesca has led to differing interpretations of what idyllic star-crossed love entails. Even Dante put the two lovers in a circle of hell, but still saw their love as a compulsion that cannot be curtailed by society.

One of the oldest love myths, as discussed previously, is the one of Pygmalion and Galatea. Captivated by that story, the Romantic painter Jean Léon Gérôme added a passionate kiss to the scenario that was missing from the original legend in his 1890 masterpiece, *Pygmalion and Galatea*. As mentioned, Pygmalion loathed all women, but he still pined for love. So, as a sculptor, he decided to carve his own image of the perfect woman out of marble, calling her Galatea. He fell instantly in love with her. During Aphrodite's annual festival of love, Pygmalion went to the love goddess's altar, imploring her to turn Galatea into a flesh and blood woman, so that he could love her completely. Aphrodite heard his heartfelt plea, granting his wish. When Pygmalion returned home he kissed Galatea, as Gerome's marvelous painting suggests, and she came to life. In true fairytale style, the two promised eternal love for each other (Fig. 5.3):

Fig. 5.3 *Pygmalion and Galatea (John Léon Gérôme, 1890)* (Wikimedia Commons)

The fascination with the ancient love myths was rekindled in the Renaissance. For example, Agnolo Bronzino's sixteenth century painting of the Cupid myth, *Venus, Cupid, Folly, and Time*, was commissioned by Cosimo de' Medici of Florence for King François I of France. In it, Venus is naked, and her son, Cupid, kisses her intimately as his arm covers her breast. Venus appears to be repelled, seeing through Cupid's capriciousness, eying him sternly. Is this folly, as the title of the painting suggests? Does it portray a kind of reversal of filial attachment, in contrast to Freud's later Oedipus complex theory? Interestingly, there is a father figure in the same scene extending his hand forward in an attempt to stop the encounter. Is this figure the voice of conscience or of guilt? Freud actually saw the conflicts recounted in mythic narratives as attempts to come to grips with unconscious psychic life. In the myth of Oedipus—the king who was abandoned at birth and unwittingly killed his father and then married his own mother—Freud discerned a narrative mirror for probing hidden sexual desires. The Bronzino painting may indeed have some Freudian echoes in it, but in a contrastive way.

One of the most passionate scenes captured on canvas is the mythic love of Hercules and Omphale, by French Rococo artist François Boucher, *Hercules and Omphale* (c. 1730). According to Greek legend, Hercules was a slave to Omphale, queen of the kingdom of Lydi. In captivity he falls desperately and irrevocably in love with her. Their affair is portrayed by Boucher as both romantic and erotic, with their arms and legs intertwined. Omphale exudes sensual power, draping her arm tantalizingly around Hercules's back, and putting her leg erotically over his. Overwhelmed, Hercules grapples her bosom. The act takes place before an audience of small cherubs. Does this suggest that the blend of *eros* and *agape* is part of some divine theater? Whatever the interpretation, Boucher's painting evokes different feelings at once, mirroring the same sense of contrast we all feel between love and lust.

A theme that emerges constantly in conceptualizations and stories of love is that of mystery; that is, of love as an existential conundrum that defies explanation but which still beckons us to decode it in our own way. Several paintings play on the mystery subtext. For example, in Francesco Hayez's 1859 magnum opus, titled *The Kiss*, we can see a man in a flowing cloak, large hat, and dark brown hair, which hide his face. The woman in the scene is only partially visible. The secret nature of romance is emphasized here, with the furtive encounter taking place in a darkly lit stairway (Fig. 5.4):

Love is selfless and nameless—the figures could be anyone, anywhere. The puzzle that such scenes suggest is why we engage in such acts spontaneously, as if we were searching to unravel some hidden secret. The same mystery theme is captured by Edvard Munch in his iconic painting, *The Kiss*

Fig. 5.4 *Il bacio (The Kiss) (by Francesco Hayez, 1859)* (Wikimedia Commons)

(1897). Two lovers are seen in an ardent embrace, but their facial features are indistinct. They could, again, be anyone, anywhere. The encounter takes place in darkness, reinforcing the mysterious nature of this act. Analogously, Magritte's painting of two lovers (*Les Amants*, 1928) whose faces are covered by a shroud similarly suggests that love poses a deep mystery that transcends individual romantic encounters, reaching deeply into the conundrum of the human condition itself. The greatest mystery of all is why there is a connection (or opposition) between sex as part of reproductive biology and love as part of human spirituality? In many of these paintings the two are intertwined and the reason for this is certainly mysterious. A very powerful portrayal of this blend is Henri Toulouse-Lautrec's controversial 1892 painting, *In Bed: The Kiss*, which shows two women kissing passionately, yet tenderly, in bed (Fig. 5.5):

Toulouse-Lautrec painted a number of other couples in bed, but described this scene as his best one. The couple is captured holding one another closely,

Fig. 5.5 *In Bed: The Kiss (Henri Toulouse-Lautrec, 1892)* (Wikimedia Commons)

as if they want this moment of unity to last forever. Lovemaking leads to spiritual unity—a true mystery if there ever was one.

Sculpture emerged in antiquity to celebrate significant events in the life of a community, generally designed to adorn the public square. The sculptures were anonymous, and considered to be part of the architecture of public places. As we saw above with the statue of Aphrodite, the art of sculpture often dealt with love and its mythological conceptualizations. This is found across cultures. In the Chitragupta Temple, dating back to circa 1000 CE in India, we find a sculpture dedicated to Surya, the Sun God and likely source of love. Having a divine source, the sculpture suggests that love descends upon us from above (the Sun God) to rule human destiny.

Sculptures across time have aimed to carve into stone the meaning of love as a shaper of human life. Antonio Canova's *Psyche Revived by Cupid's (Love's) Kiss* (1787) is a perfect example of a sculpture that portrays love as a spiritual force. Canova depicts the anticipation of a kiss between Cupid and Psyche, after Psyche had regained his love, and is under the spell of an enchanted sleep (Fig. 5.6):

The near-kiss between the two mythic lovers is expectantly intimate and tender. They gaze into one another's eyes. Psyche puts her hands on Cupid's head as he cradles her bosom with an arm. In its own way, this sculpture captures the hidden meaning of the original myth. Psyche was a beautiful woman, and this made Venus jealous. So, Venus ordered her son, Cupid, to make Psyche fall in love with the ugliest man in the world. But Cupid was the one who fell in love with Psyche. Afraid to lose her, Cupid forbade her to look at his face. When she finally did, he abandoned her. They were eventually reunited and the sculpture captures the moment of reunification.

Fig. 5.6 *Psyche Revived by Cupid's Kiss (Antonio Canova, 1787)* (Wikimedia Commons)

Fig. 5.7 *Love Dish (El Frate, c. 1550)* (Wikimedia Commons)

It is relevant to note that visual representations of love were not only the work of great artists, but also of craftsmen and business people, who aimed to make a profit from the pictography of love, starting in the Renaissance, when the equivalent of modern-day artifacts, such as "love dishes," were produced en masse for people to display as tokens (literally) of love. The one above is a typical example. It is a love dish showing a romantic couple. It was likely intended as a betrothal gift. As the man smooches the woman, he seems to be offering her a rose—the quintessential symbol of love in that era. His fingers touch her body tenderly, perhaps indicating the kind of relationship that the new couple is expected to have (Fig. 5.7):

Photographic Images

In early 1956 a young photographer named Alfred Wertheimer was assigned to take photographs of Elvis Presley, who had become a superstar rock musician of the teen culture in that era. The photo showed Elvis kissing a young woman erotically. It shocked the adult world. Nowadays, we view it with nostalgic eyes. There are two lessons to be gleaned from this event. First, what is considered obscene in one era may turn into something nostalgic in a later era. The second, and more relevant one for the present purposes, is that photography is a powerful medium, capturing those fleeting and otherwise irretrievable moments in time, extracting them from the flux of change that characterizes life. Such "captured" moments have unconscious appeal because they allow us literally to reflect upon them by "re-seeing" them. With Instagram and other new media for capturing these moments, photography is revealing itself to be our modern-day documenter of everyday life. Given the number of photos that deal with "love events," such as kissing, hugging, wedding pictures, etc., it is obvious that photography has become a major visual art for representing and capturing them.

Since the advent of photographic technology in the late nineteenth century, the art of photography has captured truly unique love events. Alfred Eisenstaedt's famous photo is certainly one of the most famous. Through the image of two people, a sailor and a nurse, kissing passionately, we can relive that special moment over and over, experiencing the passion communicated by Eisenstaedt's captured image. It is a powerful visual testimonial of love, enshrining it into communal memory (Fig. 5.8).

The photo was snapped on August 14, 1945 in Times Square in New York City, during a parade to celebrate the end of World War II. The photo was plastered all over the newspapers, becoming symbolic of a new era of peace, love, and hope. Prints of the photo are still everywhere—in households and workplaces across America. The photo captures a "Paolo and Francesca moment," as it can be called, transforming the event into a larger-than-life one. Moreover, like the cryptic kissers in the paintings discussed above, the two lovers are unknown, injecting a sense of mystery into it. But fantasy often gives way to reality, as discussed several times already. Eisenstaedt wrote subsequently that he had followed the sailor through the crowd, since he appeared

Fig. 5.8 *Alfred Eisenstaedt's famous photo (1945)* (Wikimedia Commons)

to be a Don Juan character who would kiss anyone wearing a skirt. Our famous sailor therefore turns out to be a philanderer, rather than a romantic chivalric lover, as we certainly would like to imagine him to be.

Another iconic photo is Robert Doisneau's *Le Baiser de l'Hotel de Ville* (The Kiss at City Hall), which was taken in Paris in 1950. Doisneau's images of the liberation of Paris after World War II appeared in countless newspapers and magazines throughout the world. But it is his *Baiser* photo of two lovers furtively stealing a kiss on a crowded Paris street that has become one of his most reprinted images, from postcards and posters to social media sites. What makes the photo romantic is the fact that the couple performs the kiss with closed eyes and in public. But again, fantasy seems to cede invariably to reality, since Doisneau admitted that the photo did not capture a spontaneous moment in time, but that it was actually staged. But to those who view it for the first time, the thrill of romance that a kiss evokes comes through nonetheless.

Photos are visual mementos of who we are. They have strong appeal because they provide eyewitness evidence, literally, that we exist and that our lives are meaningful. Michelangelo Antonioni's 1966 movie masterpiece, *Blow-Up*, revolves around this subtext. The story concerns the search for clues to a crime in a blow-up of a photograph. A successful photographer in the city of London, whose daily life revolves around fashion photography and easy sex, starts to realize at a certain point that his life is boring and meaningless without true love. He meets a beautiful young mysterious woman and takes photos of her incessantly, mesmerized by her beauty and wanting to capture it on photographic film. He notices something frightfully suspicious in the background of one of the photographs he took of her in a park. After studying the blow-up of the photo, he uncovers details which suggest that a murder had taken place. He goes back to the crime scene, but the body has disappeared. Bewildered, he goes through the movie searching for the body or at least an explanation of why it is not there. Neither comes. So at the end he watches a tennis match—likely in a dream—with imaginary balls being used. The image of the match slowly fades leaving only the grassy area where the presumed dead body was photographed. The unsolved crime leaves the protagonist and the viewer in a state of moral suspension, emphasizing our inability to solve life's dilemmas. Sardonically, his romantic tryst with the young woman fades as well, leaving him in a state of ambiguity—a perfect metaphor for one of the main subtexts of this book.

Pop Art Images

An image by American artist Robert Indiana, which has become highly popular and a meme in current Internet culture is *LOVE*, consisting of the capital letters L and O over V and E in bold font. The O is slanted creating a line that connects with the V, almost as if they were in some romantic embrace. Indiana's approach to *love*, which some might call conceptual art, shows how much we are fascinated by the word itself and what it tells us about ourselves. It became so well liked that it served as a print template for a Christmas card printed by the Museum of Modern Art in 1964 and, in the same year, was

Fig. 5.9 *1973 U.S. postage stamp* (Wikimedia Commons)

used by the post office for its 8-cent stamp—which has now become a prized artifact in philately (Fig. 5.9):

The image was turned into a sculpture in 1970 for the Indianapolis Museum of Art. It is now an Internet meme at Valentine's Day. While it may not be as visceral as are the paintings, sculptures, and photos discussed above, it still captures, in its own graphic way, the essence of what love entails—the letters are in red, the metaphor for passion, and the fill-in colors are blue and green, the metaphors for sadness and the promise of everlasting affection respectively.

Robert Indiana is a famous pop artist. The pop art movement emerged in the 1940s and 1950s, gaining broad appeal because its visual subjects were everyday consumer objects and themes, to which everyone could relate. One of its most prominent themes was romance and sexuality in the modern world. The late New York artist Roy Lichtenstein, for example, composed a set of comic-book paintings of the kiss and its figurative and real role human sexual relations—implying that we now perceive love in terms of new media such as comic books. His 1962 painting, titled *The Kiss*, portrays this act via a graphic novel style. The male is a pilot and the woman a highly attractive "Marilyn-Monroe-like" character, with blonde hair, a red dress, red nail polish, and bright red lipstick. Both have their eyes closed, which heightens the emotional power of the kiss. Later that year, Lichtenstein painted *Kiss II*, featuring two young people in a passionate, fiery embrace, again emphasizing the romantic power of this act. In 1964, he painted *Kiss V*, in which, again, the Marilyn-Monroe-look-alike displays her sensuous bright red lips as symbolic of her sensuality. Depending on which way the image is rotated the kiss seems to communicate parting and loss, or return and joy. As is well known, Marilyn Monroe was an American cultural icon, whose great beauty made her a famous sex symbol. But in spite of her success in films, Monroe led a tragic life. She died at the age of 36 from an overdose of sleeping pills. Since her death, she has become one of the most written-about film stars in the history of Hollywood. She has been immortalized by Andy Warhol, another great pop artist, and her look has been emulated by contemporary musical artists such as Madonna.

Pop art traces its roots to the Dada movement, which was inimical to the idyllic images of love discussed above. For example, Marcel Duchamp's, *The Bride Stripped Bare by Her Bachelors, Even*, is a work that seems to inveigh against the supposed harmony of love, stripping it down to a collection of disconnected parts (discussed briefly in Chap. 2) (Fig. 5.10):

Fig. 5.10 *The Bride Stripped Bare by Her Bachelors, Even (Marcel Duchamp, 1915–1923)* (Wikiart, Public Domain)

The work deconstructs the traditional view of romance and marriage as unifying forces. It is impossible to identify the so-called "bride" and the "bachelors" as such. They seem to be fragments and sketches that have no thematic unity. In a similar deconstructive approach to romance, in 1963 Andy Warhol filmed a group of his friends kissing in four-minute-long shots. The result was a filmic montage called *Kiss*, which shook the art world at first. New York's Gramercy Arts Theater played a new Warhol-filmed kiss each week for a while. The movie actually focuses on the anatomy of the kiss and its mysterious hold on us. The gender of the kissers is unclear, adding to the power of the act as one that transcends sexual orientation—yet another of the main subtexts of this book.

One of the lesser-known, but still one of the greatest figures in the pop art movement, was the late Keith Haring whose art recalls ancient cave art intertwined with contemporary images in a naïf style. Like Jean Dubuffet, who drew his chief inspiration from graffiti and the art produced by children and primitive cultures, Haring challenged the historically-conditioned artistic eye with his use of primordial symbols, such as "X," which stands for any "unknown," including love. The "X" is a leitmotif in many of Haring's works. At one level it may allude to the Generation X culture of the 1980s to designate an identity-less, obscure, unmotivated generation that had nowhere to go and nothing to conquer, living without goals.[9] In a 1983 work, titled "X-people," we see headless people, welcoming the computer into their lives, which is the head on a giant bug. The jarring effect that this produces can be seen in the jagged lines that emanate from the screen, producing a dissonant, strident effect on the viewer. As Marina Roy has pointed out, the symbol X taps into a complex system of meanings that reaches back to the mysterious origins of language.[10] Among the first to recognize its strange appeal was Plato, who observed in the *Timaeus* that X represented the oppositional substance of the universe in which we live. In Haring's 1983 drawing, we see the human being as a kind of Platonic X pulled in different directions by the hands and legs emanating from an unknown place (perhaps from beyond the physical world).

Maybe the X is an archetype that reverberates with mystery, a kind of chiasmus of consciousness. In one of his works, Haring shows that the X and Egyptian ankh are versions of the same archetype, placing the ankh into what appears to be a womb, suggesting the birth of human consciousness in both biological and symbolic terms. The ankh was, in fact, a symbol for both life and rebirth. It might be a stretch to interpret it and the X as symbolic of love and its connection to both critical events. But in the overall context of Haring's works, love seems to embody the contrasts that drive human life. One of these, as argued here, is the oppositional nature of the love-sex continuum and our inability to grasp why it exists in the first place. Haring brings this out in one of his most powerful paintings, which shows a *Penthouse* centerfold model, Pia Zadora, an icon of erotic culture in his era, whose sensual pose overwhelms a male figure on the side, and who seems to be undergoing electric shock, with a flag of surrender appearing in the light bulb in his head. *Eros* seems to always have an upper hand—if *agape* is missing. In a number of his other paintings we see half-human creatures engaging with each other in scatological and sexual acts, emphasizing the chaos of human emotions—a powerful visual metaphor for the love-sex opposition.

Epilogue

As discussed in this chapter, artists have dealt with both the ideal-idyllic and more profane-erotic sides of love. As discussed, satyrs were the counterparts of the love gods and goddesses; they were followers of the wine god Bacchus, hairy votaries of sex, dance and ecstasy. In Renaissance art they were portrayed as walking phalluses, embodiments of lust, who chased nymphs or sleeping goddesses. The satyr myth suggests that sexuality cannot be tamed or curtailed, no matter how much we try. Its only true antidote is romantic love, as the idyllic statues, such as the Rodin one, have always suggested. William-Adolphe Bouguereau's well-known painting, *Nymphs and Satyr* (1873), depicts how *eros* can stimulate a chaotic vortex of urges, with bodies involved in an instinctive dance of lust (Fig. 5.11):

Throughout history, art has allowed us to visualize the contrasting forces of *eros* and *agape* within us. Maybe this reflects the dual structure of the brain, its limbic and neocortical parts. We can literally "see" the moods and shades of the love-sex dichotomy through the brains of the great artists. According to Plato, the eyes of sculptors see an image in a formless slab of marble, giving it physical shape with their hands and imaginations. The resulting sculpture then provides a perspective that would otherwise have gone unnoticed. The world changes as a consequence.

The history of love as documented in images is intertwined with the history of entire societies. The ancient Greek sculptures portrayed love goddesses as powerful and defiant, and as founders of their worlds. The Greeks believed, for instance, that their civilization was founded by a woman, Athena, who sprang full-grown and armored from the forehead of the god Zeus, loved deeply by humans. As his favorite child, Zeus entrusted her with his shield and his principal weapon, the thunderbolt. Athena's temple, the Parthenon, was located in Athens, the city named after her. She wielded

Fig. 5.11 *Nymphs and Satyr (William-Adolphe Bouguereau, 1873)* (Wikimedia Commons)

enormous power over the world, becoming revered as the goddess of cities, industry, the arts, war, and wisdom.

Since antiquity, we have been both enchanted and terrified by the *eros-agape* opposition within us. One of the most terrifying images is William Blake's *Kiss of Adam and Eve*, which he drew as an illustration to John Milton's book, *Paradise Lost* (1808). In it, we see Adam looking into Eve's eyes in a state of terror and fright, seemingly asking an existential question: What is this all about? The hands that touch both personages are unidentified—they could be divine or satanic. The ambiguity and uncertainty are powerful—love is both divine and satanic, spiritual and carnal, sacred and profane (Fig. 5.12).

Fig. 5.12 *Kiss of Adam and Eve (William Blake, 1808)* (Wikimedia Commons)

As Blake seems to have grasped with the imagination of a great artist, fear may well be the originating principle in human consciousness, and the search for understanding the meaning of love the first act intended to countervail it.

Notes

1. Cited in David Wallechinsky and Amy Wallace, *The Book of Lists* (Edinburgh: Canongate Books, 2004), p. 22.
2. Denis Dutton, *The Art Instinct: Beauty, Pleasure, and Human Evolution* (London: Bloomsbury, 2009).
3. Susanne K. Langer, *Philosophy in a New Key* (New York: Mentor Books, 1948).
4. Roland Barthes, "Rhetoric of the Image," in Carolyn Handa (ed.), *Visual Rhetoric in a Visual World: A Critical Sourcebook* (New York: Bedford/St. Martin's, 2004, originally 1964).
5. John Berger, *Ways of Seeing* (Harmondsworth: Penguin, 1972).
6. Rudolph Arnheim, *Visual Thinking* (Berkeley: University of California Press, 1969).
7. Vico, *The New Science*, op. cit.
8. Donald Verene, *Vico's Science of Imagination* (Ithaca: Cornell University Press, 1981), p. 101.
9. Douglas Coupland, *Generation X* (New York: St. Martin's, 1991).
10. Marina Roy, *Sign After the X* (Vancouver: Advance Artspeak, 2000).

6

Love Symbols and Rituals

Homo sapiens is the species that invents symbols in which to invest passion and authority, then forgets that symbols are inventions.
—Joyce Carol Oates (b. 1938)

Prologue

Traditionally, cultures have marked the coming-of-age phase of life in various symbolic and ritualistic ways, including the use of facial decorations and the giving of gifts in the service of courtship customs. Even in modern-day urban cultures, cosmetic industries are contemporary reflexes of ancient practices that are based on the symbolism of love and fertility. The colors used in lipsticks and eye decorations, as well as the rings people put on their ears, nose, lips, eyebrows, and tongue are artifacts that are intended to enhance some aspect of appearance or to signal some inherent perception of the meaning of courtship and romance. They are embedded in historical traditions, resonating with ancient meanings, but updated to fit a modern context. Symbolism is, therefore, yet another semiotic key for decoding the meaning of love in human life.[1]

Returning to Popper's Worlds 1, 2, and 3 model of meaning-making, it can be said that love symbols and activities are abstractions (World 2) of bodily impulses (World 1) that become set over time in communal perception as meaningful constructs of romance (World 3). So, for example, the kiss is arguably a reaction (World 2) to impulses (World 1) that has been enshrined

© The Author(s) 2019
M. Danesi, *The Semiotics of Love*, Semiotics and Popular Culture,
https://doi.org/10.1007/978-3-030-18111-6_6

over time into a symbolic act of romance via poetry, narratives, paintings, sculptures, etc. (World 3). The origin of the love-as-sweetness metaphor (Chap. 3) can perhaps be connected to the pleasant gustatory sense of sweetness that seems to crystallize on our lips when kissing our loved one. The act and its sensory-metaphorical interpretation have produced a set of derived symbols and rituals that would otherwise be unthinkable without this conceptualization. Since the medieval period, in fact, selected food items that have a sweet taste, such as chocolates, have become part of love rituals, such as the giving of sweets at Valentine's Day. According to a French custom of the medieval era, when the moon went through its phases the romantic couple was expected to drink a brew called *metheglin*, which was made from honey. From this we eventually developed the modern-day notion of a *honeymoon*, or the belief that a period of romance after marriage was critical for the lovers to strengthen the knot that they tied at marriage, in a pleasant metaphorically-saccharine way. The original idea of a "honeymoon" period actually comes from ancient Babylonia when newlyweds were expected to be alone for a period of a month, so that they could get a head start on procreation; but the actual metaphor of love-as-a-sweet taste starts in the chivalric era. In that same era, as we saw, the rose also became symbolic of love since, by association, it is a flower that produces a sweet smell. It is thus a small cognitive leap to associate it with the love-as-a-sweet-taste concept. When viewed semiotically in this way, we can now plausibly explain the giving of chocolates and roses in the enactment of love during Valentine's Day as a consequence of previous symbolic processes.

This brief semiotic excursion into the romantic meanings of three symbols—the kiss, chocolate, and roses—is intended to bring out the fact that the symbols and rituals of love-making are tied to our perceptions and experiences of love. We enshrine these into communal practices and celebrations to produce an overall code for conducting love-based events and practices. Incidentally, aware of the metaphorical-gustatory link between chocolate and kisses an Italian candy manufacturer (Perugina) has become famous for its *Baci* products (meaning "kisses"). Inside each individually-wrapped chocolate a little poem or proverb related to love and romance can be found. The little chocolate is thus packed with historical semiotic meaning and intent, combining poetry (the language of love) with a cultural metaphor (the view that love is connected to sweetness).

The love practices that revolve around sweetness as a love concept, such as the giving of chocolate and roses to a paramour, gain momentum only if they are truly meaningful to a group or society, thus suggesting that some archetypal or universal sense-making process is involved, connecting the body (through taste) to the emotions and sense-making generally. These may, of course, contrast with other conceptualizations and practices, such as ancient fertility and courtship rituals that emphasized sexual control and fertility, rather than romance. Marriage in pre-civilized groups was often conducted by the capture or barter of women, not through romantic choice, especially if there existed a scarcity of nubile women within a particular village, whereupon men in one village would go and raid other villages for wives. As civilizations came onto the evolutionary scene, this type of "marriage hunting" gave way primarily to arranged marriages, a tradition that extended well into the early medieval period, when marriages were primarily transactions between families so as to assure financial security or else to forge certain political alliances—a practice which continues in some parts of the world to this day.

Love customs, with their symbols and rituals, may seem strange to outsiders. But to those reared in the cultures that utilize them they have great emotional and socially-stabilizing power. Take, as an example, the ancient tradition in Nordic countries of a young woman wearing an empty sheath on her belt as part of the courtship period. A suitor interested in her romantically would put a knife in the sheath, which she would then wear, if she so wanted, as a sign of betrothal. This may seem strange today, reverberating with phallic overtones, but it really is not much different than giving a diamond ring to a paramour to signify betrothal. It is the act of giving that is universal; not what is given. All such rituals symbolize the notion of love as a "tie that binds." They may look strange on the surface, but below they constitute analogous sign structures that indicate the universal perception of love as a binding force.

Symbols of Love

As mentioned above and in a previous chapter, the rose has symbolized romantic love since the era of courtly love. Roses can be of various colors, of course. But red is the most common one, arguably because it is the color of blood thus implying an unconscious metaphorical connection of love to fertility and life. The source of blood is the heart and this might explain why the heart itself is considered a symbol for love across time and cultures. The ancient Egyptians saw the heart organ as the seat of the love feeling. Ancient alchemists believed that the heart beat in synch with the rhythms of love, hence its use as symbolic of this emotion. As Diane Ackerman writes, "Throughout history, people have located love in the heart, probably because of its loud, safe, and comforting beat."[2] This explains why jewelry, boxes of chocolates, love cards, etc. given at Valentine's often come in the shape of a heart. A common version of this symbol is a heart pierced by an arrow, an

Fig. 6.1 *Heart pierced by an arrow symbol of love* (Wikimedia Commons)

image suggesting both that love pierces us through the heart and that once pierced we cannot escape its fate, imbuing it with a latent mythological meaning that recalls the Cupid myth (Fig. 6.1):

The heart symbol, incidentally, is one of the most common ones used in everyday emoji communications.[3] Its various colors and shades involve nuances and subtleties of meaning that have metaphorical sources. So, for instance the red heart expresses love or friendship, while the yellow heart is a friendship sign. The broken heart emoji shows the loss of love or the feeling of missing a loved one, whereas the beating heart with vibration lines represents an exciting love life. The list of variants could go on and on.

The heart symbol is intertwined with metaphorical reasoning, implying an inter-hemispheric neurological source (right versus left hemispheres), as the classic experiment by Winner and Gardner showed in 1977.[4] The two researchers presented a series of verbal metaphors to various subjects asking them to select one of four response pictures which best portrayed the meaning of the metaphors. For the sentence "A heavy heart can really make a difference" the subjects were shown four pictures from which to choose: (1) a person crying (= metaphorical meaning); (2) a person staggering under the weight of a huge red heart (= literal meaning); (3) a 500-pound weight (= a representation emphasizing the adjective *heavy*); (4) a red heart (= a representation emphasizing the noun phrase *red heart*). The subjects were divided into aphasics (subjects with damage to the left hemisphere), patients with right hemisphere damage, and a normal control group. The latter gave five times as many correct metaphorical responses; but the right hemisphere patients could respond only with equal frequency to both the metaphorical and literal cues. Winner and Gardner thus established a link between the meaning of a metaphor and the right hemisphere of the brain, making it possible to hypothesize by extrapolation that the heart symbol reverberates with suggestive imagery and intuitive sense—both functions of the right hemisphere.

In its physical-visual representational form the heart symbol is more precisely an icon. As discussed previously (Chap. 2), an icon represents its referent through resemblance. As the heart symbol indicates, many symbols may start out as icons, but they end up being interpreted in specific symbolic and indexical ways. So, the heart symbol is an icon of the heart organ, but is interpreted as representing romantic love because of the history behind the perceptions of the heart as the love organ. It is also an index, since it points conceptually to a presumed location of the love emotion. But the iconic and indexical qualities of the heart sign are understood by convention, that is, in situations where they are assigned the meaning of love. In this sense, the heart is a symbol. Actually, according to some, the heart symbol is hardly representative of the heart organ, claiming that it probably originated in the realm of *eros*, representing the shape of women's buttocks. Whether or not this is verifiable, it is clear that today we do not see sexual imagery in the heart symbol, unless it is pointed out to us, and even then we tend to be skeptical.

The spread of the heart as a symbol of love gained diffusion in the medieval courtly love era. The painting below is the first known visual representation of the heart symbol. It appeared in an anonymous thirteenth century French manuscript titled *Roman de la poire* (Romance of the Pear), in which a romantic suitor is offering his heart to a paramour on his knees (Fig. 6.2)[5]:

Fig. 6.2 *Illustration for "Roman de la poire" (thirteenth century)* (Wikimedia Commons)

The expression "to give your heart to someone" is the linguistic-metaphorical counterpart to this image, indicating that we perceive love as a precious (life-preserving) object that, when given, ties us physically and spiritually to the person receiving the heart. The concept that there was one and only one love is also embedded in this image since, by logical exclusion, once the heart is given it cannot be retrieved easily. Interestingly, the heart symbol was adopted by the Church as a symbol of Christ's love for humanity, that is, as a "sacred heart." Christ's heart is shown as giving off divine light, enveloped by a crown of thorns, and bleeding because it is pierced by a lance—all symbolic of the Crucifixion. Indirectly the use of the heart as a symbol of romance and religion suggests that the two were likely perceived to be intertwined spiritually.

In addition to the heart, chocolate became attached symbolically to the experience of love right after it was introduced to Europe in the fifteenth century. Chocolate originated among the Aztecs and the Maya, whose hieroglyphs indicate that they considered it to be a sexual stimulant, purportedly enhancing the male's sexual prowess. Chocolate was brought to Europe around 1519 by the Spaniards. There it became a gustatory luxury of the upper classes, becoming symbolic of romance after Princess Maria Theresa gave it as an engagement gift to Louis XIV, believing that it had aphrodisiac qualities. The 2000 movie *Chocolat*, based on the 1999 novel by Joanne Harris, brings out this historical tradition effectively. The story revolves around a young mother who settles into a small French village with her six-year-old daughter, opening a *chocolaterie*. The chocolate she sells or gives to people changes their lives. It rekindles romance in an older couple; a man is given courage to approach his secret love; and many other romantic events are traced to the *chocolaterie*. This is a modern-day myth and fairytale packed into a single narrative, with the owner of the store a contemporary Aphrodite.

Although we now associate it with sweetness, the word *chocolate* actually comes from an indigenous word meaning "bitter water." This is due to the fact that the fruit of the cacao tree is actually sour. Fermentation and the addition of sugar give cacao the sweet taste that we associate with chocolate. It is relevant to note that the chocolates symbolizing love must be of a certain, and generally smaller, size. A large chocolate, such as a chocolate candy bar, is hardly interpreted as a gift involving romance or love. It is perceived as a palatable treat, and classified culturally with other kinds of "junk food."

Another symbolic love object with ancient roots is the finger ring, which has been part of love traditions across the world and across time.[6] Archeologists trace the ring back to prehistoric times, when inserting it into a finger seemingly had fertility symbolism. Rings given to a paramour indicating fidelity, rather than fertility, were first exchanged in Egypt around 3000 years ago.

Egyptian scrolls reveal that they were worn on the third finger of the left hand, since it was believed that the vein in that finger ran directly into the heart. The rings were initially made from papyrus reeds. The men gave them to the women as a symbol of their eternal commitment to them—including in the afterlife. Since the papyrus rings did not last long, they were eventually replaced with bands made from bone or ivory. In Roman times, rings were made from durable materials, such as iron. Like the Greeks, the Romans put the ring on the fourth finger of the left hand, believing that this finger contained the *vena amoris*, or the vein of love. The custom of exchanging gold wedding rings comes from 860 CE, when Pope Nicholas I made it compulsory for wedding bands to be made of this metal to ensure that the groom's commitment was financial as well as amorous. Diamond rings became part of courtship practices among the nobility starting in 1477 when Mary of Burgundy was the first aristocrat to receive a diamond engagement ring from her fiancé, the Holy Roman Emperor, Maximilian I. For those who could afford it, the diamond ring spread as a symbol of eternal love in modernity—a subtext that underlies the "Diamonds are Forever" slogan of the De Beers diamond company, a marketing strategy linking love, marriage, and diamonds, starting with the company's 1948 marketing campaign. Recently, De Beers attempted to detach the meaning of the diamond ring from this tradition with a new marketing slogan—"Women of the world raise your right hand," mirroring the working class slogan "Workers of the world, unite," suggesting that by putting the ring on the right hand, rather than the left, women could declare their independence from the past in a symbolic way. However, this slogan was quickly abandoned and the original one reinstated, suggesting that in love and marriage the theme of unity, not independence, is etched into our cultural DNA.

During the sixteenth and seventeenth centuries, gimmal rings became popular as betrothal symbols, indicating union materially since the ring was made up of two interlocking parts. After the engagement, each partner wore one part and, at the wedding ceremony, the groom would place his part on the bride's finger, reuniting the set as representative of binding the two partners in permanent love (Fig. 6.3).

Interestingly, in Puritan Colonial America, the groom would give the spouse a thimble, because jewelry was seen as frivolous. The bride would remove the top of the thimble to create a ring. Again, love, marriage, and religion seem to be intertwined, no matter what era or what religious belief system. What matters is the meaning of lovers as spiritual partners, or "soul mates," as the English expression goes, thus connecting romance with religious traditions. The counterparts to rings are so-called love knots

Fig. 6.3 *Gimmal ring (British Museum)* (Wikimedia Commons)

made of ribbons. The origin of the knots is uncertain. There is little doubt, however, that they too are intended to symbolize eternal union, representing it through the winding, intertwining loops that have neither a beginning nor an end, much like a Möbius strip. Our expression "to tie the knot" to signal marriage derives from this symbolic practice.

No discussion of love symbols can ignore the meaning of stars in love-making, as indicated previously in the discussion of the stories of star-crossed lovers. The stars connect love to metaphysical forces, transcending its biological function. The origin of astrology itself is an attempt to explain magical forces in life, such as love, and their connection to some hidden code of destiny that is "written" in the stars. Once smitten, there is no way out of it, no matter what one's age, gender, or social status. The heart leads the mind, it would seem, even if there are great risks involved. To this day, prospective love mates might go to a fortune teller to seek advice on their love lives, not to mention read the horoscope to glean insights about their romantic future. These are residual behaviors of the perceived magic of love that goes back to the ancient myths where divine forces dictated its course and outcomes. The continued popularity of astrology in matters of love actually implies that we sense unconsciously that there might be a mystical "master code" that guides human destiny. Although we might see this as a superstitious belief today, we hardly realize that the giving of roses, rings, and other symbolic love artifacts has similar mythical-mystical origins. Newspapers in England began publishing daily horoscope columns during the 1930s. Similar columns soon appeared in newspapers throughout the world, as modern-day people became increasingly interested in astrology. Maybe the unconscious feeling that the stars rule the passions is part of our collective unconscious—a carryover from prehistory. Whether this is true or not is actually beside the point. The fact is that we humans do not make love only to reproduce ourselves biologically, but to connect ourselves to each other and to the cosmos. This topic will broached in the next chapter.

There are an infinite number of symbolic objects and artifacts throughout the world's cultures that are connected with love. In human life, there is virtually no object that is not imbued with meaning, because we perceive objects as signs that evoke a broad range of meanings. Objects such as rings, chocolates, knots, heart artifacts, and so on cohere into a system of signification that mirrors, in microcosm, the sensory and emotional structures associated with love. They are physical sign structures, providing valuable clues as to what love is all about in human terms. Especially significant are those that are thought to possess mysterious powers. This includes the stars and chocolate, among others, as we have seen. This kind of symbolism is the basis of the ancient craft of alchemy, defined as the art of transmuting materials that lasted well into the medieval ages and that continues to have some adherents to this day. The principal activity of the alchemists was the search for the "philosopher's stone"—popularized as a unique object by the highly popular Harry Potter movies of the early 2000s—and the production of gold by artificial means. Gold meant (and continues to mean) power, deification, and immortality. A gold ring certainly seems to reverberate latently with this meaning.

There is a common belief throughout the world that objects are not only signs standing for conventional social meanings, but that they also possess some inner force above and beyond the physical. In some societies belief in the powers of objects is so strong that it develops into the belief system called *animism*—the view that spirits inhabit or communicate with humans through material objects. Latent animism is certainly a semiotic force in many of the love objects described here. This is perhaps why we put so much meaning in rings and other love artifacts—they seem to have an animistic quality to them. Love itself seems to have an *anima*, a soul, that is injected into us either mythologically (from Cupid's arrows), or through the body's emotional system, animating the soul.

XOXO

Two symbols that require special semiotic treatment are X and O, which have been used for centuries to represent the "kiss" and the "hug" respectively in written communications—that is, XOXO now means "hugs and kisses." The most plausible hypothesis for the origin of X as a symbol of the kiss comes from medieval practices, when X was a sign representing Christianity and thus a sign of faith, fidelity, and Christian love. The X was a letter-abbreviation of the Greek word for Christos, Χρῆστος. It was used by religious authorities and the nobility as a common seal in official correspondences, based on its sacred meaning, and thus constituting the likely source for the expression "sealed with a kiss," since the X was added to a seal embossed in wax or some other substance after it was licked with the lips (the organs of osculation). When kissing became an act of romantic love in the same era, enshrined into the communal imagination with stories such as the Paolo and Francesca one, it is plausible to argue that it became the sign for "sealing" love affairs.

How and when the O was added to the XOXO greeting or salutation is unknown. One can only speculate, by connecting it to the meaning of circles in various cultural traditions, since the hug is iconic of the circle itself. The circle has been a symbol of perfection and infinity since antiquity. This is probably due to the fact that its shape suggests eternal recurrence. As such, it is an archetype that shows up in many spiritual traditions, including ancient sacred geometry, which ascribes symbolic and metaphysical meanings to certain geometric shapes and certain geometric proportions. It is based on the belief that the divinities are the master geometers of the world. So, it could well be that the hug is perceived not only as iconically representative of the circle, but also as something sacred whose meaning transcends this physical action.

As a symbol, X has, actually, many meanings: it is the common variable symbol in algebra; it is the signature used by those who cannot write; it is a sign of danger when put on bottles of alcohol or boxes of dynamite; it is a symbol marking treasure on a pirate's map; and so on and so forth.[7] In Robert Priest's 1984 novel titled *The Man Who Broke Out of the Letter X*, the obsession with danger and excitement is palpable and deadly.[8] The same lethal mixture is found in the X-File series of television programs and in movie characters such as agent Triple XXX. As Marina Roy puts it: "Most cultural and linguistic investments in the letter X carry the grain of something inherently fatal."[9]

Like the rest of our alphabet, X originates in the ancient Phoenician writing system of around 1000 BCE as the letter pronounced *samekh*, meaning "fish," and used for the consonant sound S. Although relatively few words begin with X in English, the letter crops up over and over as a symbol, rather than a phonetic sign. Craig Conley has identified seventy-six distinct uses of this letter, making it one of the most versatile symbols in the English language.[10] As a symbol for Christ, the X can be seen to represent a cross form rotated 45 degrees. Diverse groups of Christians have adopted different styles of crosses. Roman Catholics and Protestants use the Latin cross, made with a vertical straight line with a shorter horizontal crosspiece above the center (to resemble the cross on which Christ died). Eastern Orthodox Churches use the Greek cross, instead, which has four arms of equal length. Cross figures have also been found in Nordic cultures, dating before Christian times, in rock engravings from about 800 BCE. It is a chiasmus sign that bears many ambiguous meanings.[11]

In effect, X is a symbol that invokes mystery and sacredness, profanity and spirituality at once—a perfect oppositional blend for a semiotic theory of love. Among the first to recognize its strange appeal was Plato, who observed in the *Timaeus* that X probably represented the substance of the very universe in which we live.[12] Although he did not elaborate upon his idea, it does indeed seem to strike a resounding chord within us to this day as we look at, and use, this enigmatic character. The vertical cross sign (a sign made up of a vertical straight line crossed by a horizontal one at right angles) has been used since prehistoric times to evoke the sacred. But so too has the diagonal cross. The apostle Andrew, not feeling worthy of being executed on the upright cross like his Master, is said to have asked for crucifixion on the diagonal cross. The cross figure, as Liungman aptly points out, "stands for death and sorrow and their opposites: eternal life and salvation," and, thus, the sacred dimension in human understanding.[13] The diagonal cross produces, as does any modification of a form, an opposition, as discussed throughout this book. Like the yin and yang of ancient Chinese philosophy, it would seem that we perceive the world's most basic relations as a balancing act between two opposing life forces—the sacred and the profane.[14]

Modern day marketing practices have actually provided a new channel for expressing the ancient dualism embedded in the X form. As Sacks puts it: "X has been drafted for marketing and advertising; it now signifies something like 'computer magic and control' or 'cutting edge'."[15] Magic is indeed something that X suggests unconsciously, and thus a perfect emblem of love itself.

Love Rituals

Ritual weaves a feeling of magic on groups, binding them together in a sense of stability and meaningfulness. As discussed above, the exchange of rings is a common courtship, betrothal, and marriage ritual, thus connecting the symbolism of the ring to attendant rituals of love and romance and, by extension, to a sense of social bonding between the love partners and the social milieu in which the ritual takes place. Rather than a ring, in parts of Africa, brides are expected to wear necklaces or ankle bracelets instead, and these, like rings, are given or exchanged in ritualistic ceremonies of love and marriage.

As mentioned, love and courtship rituals and customs may seem strange to cultural outsiders. But to those reared in situations that utilize and enact them they have great emotional power. In seventeenth century Wales, ornate "love-spoons" were given by a suitor to a young woman to show his love towards her. While this might seem strange, it has nevertheless left its semiotic residues in modern-day gift-giving. We now give such spoons as gifts to celebrate weddings, anniversaries, and the birth of babies—all of which are connected to love. In eighteenth-century England, suitors sent gloves, rather than spoons, to a prospective partner. If the woman wore the gloves to church, it signaled her acceptance of the proposal. In some traditional African cultures, blades of grass are braided together and used to tie the hands of the groom and bride together to symbolize their union. All such rituals recognize the idea of love as a "tie that binds," suggesting that there is a universal semiotic substratum to all these rituals.

Love gloves actually have a fascinating story of flirtation behind them, as Geri Walton has documented in an interesting blog entry that is worth discussing here, since it brings out the relation between an object and romance in a semiotic way.[16] According to writings and documents of the nineteenth century, the specific ways in which the gloves were worn or displayed constituted a veritable love code, including the following signals and cues:

- Biting the tips of the gloves indicated that the woman wished to be rid of the paramour.
- Clenching the gloves in the right hand was an outright rejection of the suitor.
- Drawing the gloves halfway on the left hand was a sign of indifference.
- Dropping the gloves meant that she was romantically interested.
- Putting one of the tips to the lips constituted the question, "Do you love me?"
- Holding the gloves in the right hand with the thumb exposed was an invitation to be kissed.
- Putting on the gloves was a sign of anger towards the suitor.
- Smoothing them out gently indicated a wish to be with the suitor
- Striking them over a hand was a sign of displeasure.
- Striking them over the shoulder was a sign to accompany or escort her.
- Tapping the chin with the gloves indicated that she loved someone else.
- Turning the gloves inside out was a sign of total rejection.
- Twirling the gloves around the fingers was a signal to be discreet since they were being observed.

A practice also starting in eighteenth-century England, in which a brightly-decorated mistletoe in the shape of a ball would be hung at Christmastime in a doorway for purposes of prospective romance, is connected symbolically to the mistletoe itself, which symbolizes life that does not end at physical death. It is thus another symbolic manifestation of the eternity of love theme in many rituals. If a woman stood under the ornament, either by happenstance or by design, the nearest suitor was expected to kiss her, in anticipation of a potential romantic rendezvous. This ritual still exists today in some sectors of society, even if we may no longer be aware of its original connotations.

Astrology also plays a role in the ritualization of love, as discussed briefly above. The belief that the moon looks down upon lovers, especially forlorn ones, is a common one. Early peoples thought the moon was a powerful love god or goddess. The ancient Romans called her Luna and the Greeks Artemis. The early Egyptians honored a male moon god called Khonsu. The Babylonians called their moon god Sin, the most powerful of the sky gods. Some American Native societies believe that the moon and the sun were once brother and sister gods. Many have written about the moon and its effects on love partners. In *A Midsummer Night's Dream*, Shakespeare compared the moon to "a silver bow new-bent in heaven." Wild things happen when there is a full moon, and unlike love under the stars, love in the moonlight almost always conveys sadness, betrayal, or some other "lunatic" state. The word *lunatic*, incidentally, originally meant "moonstruck," and may be the source of the conceptual metaphor of love-as-a-madness (discussed previously) which goes right back to antiquity.

In Plato's *Phaedrus*, we read that Socrates, his teacher, explained love as a kind of madness, at the same time that it is a great divine gift.[17] The same metaphor took on negative social connotations in nineteenth century England, as Helen Small has so cogently argued.[18] Like Foucault, who sees notions of sexuality, and especially of sexual orientation, as part of past misguided clinical stereotypes,[19] such as the belief that different sexual orientations were pathological, rather than simple options, Small examines the figure of the love-mad woman in Romantic literature, as a fictional coalescence of this ancient metaphorical idea, turned into a stereotype. British doctors and novelists of the eighteenth and nineteenth centuries portrayed women's passions as a form of insanity. Medical and fictional stories about women who go insane when they lose their paramours were common during the era, thus portraying women's love-mad passions as an extension of the female condition.

The same metaphor is still common and directing even the neuroscience of love, which explains love as a kind of craving that can lead someone to "lose control," and thus make people do bizarre things. Some even see it as an addiction, akin to any addiction caused by drugs. But what all this misses is that our metaphorical portrayals of love as a form of insanity are simply a rationalization, an attempt to use language to explain or justify romantic behaviors. Love is involuntary, not an aberration. When the ancient Greeks characterized love as "a madness of the gods," the notion stuck, and recycled by pseudo-science.

Peculiar rituals and events connected with romance abound. These are not just prospective mating exercises, as Darwin observed.[20] Courtship rituals indicate that there is more to love than mate assessment or success at copulation. In human life, courtship is a trial period that involves the love-sex opposition in a constant emotional tug within the partners. There are various types of courtship practices. One is a controlled or chaperoned form, where the prospective marriage partners are kept apart physically but expected to interact socially under some form of supervision. A second type is somewhat similar but freer, since it is still arranged by families, but in which the lovers are allowed private time together. Spontaneous courtships, such as those that characterize modern-day dating and even hook-up practices, are probably the most common ones today. Young lovers are even expected to date different partners before settling on a mate. But this type of courtship is not historically unique. Among the Kreung peoples of Cambodia, it was common for parents of pubescent girls to build a "love hut," in which she could be left alone with different boys, in order to "test" them out. Given the spread of a global culture and its basis in a monolithic worldwide perception of courtship, these huts have virtually disappeared. An analogous tradition exists among the Zulu people. It is during the latter phases of courtship that the family of a Zulu girl builds a hut where she can meet her paramour at night. The Zulus and the Kreung actually value a long-lasting marriage—hence the huts that permit a meaningful mate search before the permanence of marriage.

Valentine's Day

One of the most widely-known love rituals of all is Valentine's Day, whose origins have been explained in various ways. One of these is the Roman celebration of the *Lupercalia* (the feast of *Lupercus*, the wolf hunter) on the fourteenth of February so as to ensure protection from wolves. During the celebration, young men were expected to strike young women with hide strips, in the belief that the woman who was best able to withstand the blows was the fertile one. As a brutal ritual, it certainly seems far removed from the

Valentine's Day occasion of today; but the blows were likely to be more meta-phorical than real, representing the wolf-like sexual urges seen to be part of masculinity. The semiotic connection between wolves and romance or sex is not a far-fetched one, as discussed previously. Wolves howl at night to send out mating calls. It is a small step from this observation to the metaphorical conceptualization of love-mates as sending and responding to love signals under the moon.

Another origin legend is the one associated with St. Valentine, a martyr of the early Christian Church around 250 CE. At the time, the Roman Emperor Claudius II forbade young men to marry, because he needed them to give up their lives to the military. A priest named Valentine disobeyed the emperor's order and secretly married young couples. For this, he was imprisoned and, while in jail, he fell in love with the jailor's blind daughter, who miraculously regained her sight through his prayerful intercession. On the night before his execution, on February 14 (according to some accounts), Valentine wrote a letter to his beloved, signing it "From Your Valentine," an episode that some historians see as the origin of the Valentine card. This legend is believed to have established February 14 as symbolic of romantic love in honor of St. Valentine. One of the most famous of all love cards was sent by Charles, the Duke of Orleans, in 1415 when he too was in prison in the Tower of London. He sent it to his wife. It is on display today at the British Museum. The card contained a passionate poem that praises love.

A third story links Valentine's Day to an old English belief that birds choose their mates on February 14. Chaucer wrote in *The Parliament of Fowls*:

> For this was on St. Valentine's Day,
> When every fowl cometh there to choose his mate.

Maybe it is from Chaucer that we got the expression "love birds," as sug-gested by his statement. In the end, it is not possible to determine which origin story is the correct one for Valentine's Day. The relevant thing to note is that most of the symbols, objects, poetic forms, and rituals discussed in this chapter converge at Valentine's Day, forming a text in the semiotic sense—that is, something that consists of parts that cohere structurally and conceptu-ally into an overall meaning. Chocolates, roses, friendship rings (often in the shape of a heart), and other romantic accouterments are essential to this text. The relation between the composition of a text and its interpretation is, actu-ally, a primary area of research within semiotics. Especially interesting is the "location" of a text's meaning. Does it lie in the intentions of the makers of texts? And, consequently, is successful interpretation of the text on the part of "readers" a straightforward matter of trying to determine the maker's intentions? The late semiotician Umberto Eco wrote at length on this very fascinating topic, suggesting that although infinite interpretations of the same text are possible, in reality the nature of the text itself constrains the range of interpretations.[21] When a given interpretation goes beyond this range, people tend to evaluate it as erroneous, extreme, far-fetched, or implausible.

The Valentine's Day text is not "written," of course, like a novel or a recipe; it has crystallized from historical practices which are connected through intertexuality—a notion introduced formally into semiotics by Roland Barthes and elaborated subsequently by Julia Kristeva.[22] As Barthes pointed out, a text is constituted by bits and pieces of signs and other texts, various conventional formulas, and specific kinds of discourses, all of which pass into the text and reconfigured within it. For Barthes the text is, thus, a blend of unconscious or automatic quotations, without quotation marks.[23] For Kristeva, too, a text is more than the result of a singular intentional effort—it is the result of other texts converging on it through historical forces. In the case of the Valentine's Day text, we do not read it in any literal sense; we perform it by enacting its components in real ways (giving roses, bringing chocolates, etc.).

Love texts and their ritualistic enactment emerge to allow humans everywhere to solve similar physical and moral problems, as the Polish-born British anthropologist Bronislaw Malinowski argued persuasively.[24] Malinowski saw the languages, rituals, and institutions that humans have created, no matter how strange they might at first seem, as possessing universal properties that have permitted people everywhere to resolve or cope with similar life problems. The British anthropologist Alfred Radcliffe-Brown noted that even a physical response like weeping could hardly be explained in purely biological terms.[25] Among the Andaman Islanders, in the east Bay of Bengal, he found that it was not primarily an expression of joy or sorrow, but rather a ritualistic response to social situations characterizing such meaningful events as peace-making, marriage, and the reunion of long-separated intimates. In crying together, the people renewed their ties of cultural solidarity. This line of argumentation can be applied clearly to the Valentine's Day text. It allows people a way to confront the meaning of love in everyday life, attempting to cope with its effects through symbolism and ritualization. More importantly, it acknowledges that love is a critical force in human life. Should a ritual such as Valentine's Day disappear or fade from social life, it would indicate that our views of love are morphing radically.

Epilogue

The importance of love symbols and rituals cannot be overstated—these coalesce semiotically to inform us about the love-sex dichotomy as it plays out in specific ways, that is, in terms of an Apollonian (*agape*) versus Dionysian (*eros*) symbolic opposition—a fact captured eloquently by the Jungian scholar Joseph L. Henderson in his classic study of initiation rites and other crucial social rituals. He puts it as follows[26]:

> The symbols that influence many vary in their purpose. Some men need to be aroused, and experience their initiation in the violence of a Dionysiac "thunder rite." Others need to be subdued, and they are brought to submission in the ordered design of temple precinct or sacred cave, suggestive of the Apollonian religion of later Greece. A full initiation embraces both themes, as we can see when we look either at the material drawn from ancient texts or at living subjects. But it is quite certain that the fundamental goal of initiation lies in taming the original Trickster-like wildness of the juvenile nature. It therefore has a civilizing or spiritualizing purpose, in spite of the violence of the rites that are required to set this process in motion.

The meaning of love can be examined not only in terms of how we have encoded its senses in words, written about it in narratives and myths, depicted it in paintings and sculptures, but also in how we have symbolized and ritualized it through the ages. Even in an age where we can get anything we want with the click of a computer mouse or a quick touch of the screen on a mobile device, we still are fascinated by the mystery of love and romance. With our gadgets and expedient relationships, we still pursue love as passionately as at any time in the past. This is why we preserve and continue to utilize historical symbols and rituals to acknowledge its universality throughout history. The sociologist Emile Durkheim saw symbolism as critical for the survival of a group, because it produces solidarity through a replication of existing cultural forms.[27] Ritual is the first phase in achieving replication and thus obtaining consensus to the cause from new recruits.[28] It thus recreates the identity of the cultural member, fashioning it in conformity to the expectations of the group. The objective is to impart to the participant a belief system and role as part of a community, as well as how the person is supposed to relate to others.

From the beginning of time, people have created symbols and rituals to help them understand the world. The Greeks symbolized the sun as the god Helios driving a flaming chariot across the sky; Egyptians represented the sun as a boat. In Babylonian myth, the hero Gilgamesh searched for a magical herb that made all who ate it immortal. Symbols stand for the phenomena of everyday life and transform them into abstractions, bearing great meaning. They assign a memorable form to events in the world, requiring no theory or explanatory science to grasp their meaning. They speak their own form of unconscious language. The symbols and rituals of love tap into this language in a powerful way.

Notes

1. For the power of symbols in human life, see Ernst Cassirer, *An Essay on Man* (New Haven: Yale University Press, 1944), *Language and Myth* (New York: Dover, 1946), and *The Philosophy of Symbolic Forms* (New Haven: Yale University Press, 1957).
2. Diane Ackerman, *Natural History of the Senses* (New York: Vintage, 1991), p. 145.
3. Marcel Danesi, *The Semiotics of Emoji: The Rise of Visual Language in the Internet Age* (London: Bloomsbury, 2016).
4. Ellen Winner and Howard Gardner, "The Comprehension of Metaphor in Brain–Damaged Patients," *Brain* 100 (1977): 717–729.
5. See P. Vinken, "How the Heart was Held in Medieval Art," *The Lancet* 358 (2001): 2155–2157.
6. See, for example, Diana Scarisbrick, *Rings: Symbols of Wealth, Power and Affection* (New York: Abrams, 1993).
7. Marina Roy, *Sign After the X* (Vancouver: Advance Artspeak, 2000).
8. Robert Priest, *The Man Who Broke Out of the Letter X* (Toronto: Coach House Press, 1984).
9. Roy, op. cit., p. 28.
10. Craig Conley, *One Letter Words* (New York: HarperCollins, 2005), pp. 203–214.
11. Jamin Pelkey, *The Semiotics of X* (London: Bloomsbury, 2017), p. 120.
12. Conley, *One Letter Words*, op. cit., p. 212.
13. Carl G. Liungman, *Dictionary of Symbols* (New York: W. W. Norton & Company, 1991), p. 10.
14. Ibid., p. 46.
15. David Sacks, *Language Visible: Unraveling the Mystery of the Alphabet from A to Z* (Toronto: Knopf, 2003), pp. 343–344.
16. Geri Walton, "Gloves and Flirting Language," Unique Histories from the 18th and 19th Centuries, Posted February 14, 2014. https://www.geriwalton.com/gloves-and-flirting-language/.
17. Plato, *Phaedrus* (Cambridge: Cambridge University Press, 1972).

18. Helen Small, *Love's Madness: Medicine, the Novel, and Female Insanity, 1800–1865* (Oxford: Oxford University Press, 1998).

19. Foucault, *The History of Sexuality*, op. cit.

20. Charles Darwin, *The Origin of Species* (New York: Collier, 1859); *The Descent of Man* (New York: Modern Library, 1871).

21. Umberto Eco, *The Role of the Reader. Explorations in the Semiotics of Texts* (Bloomington: Indiana University Press, 1979); *Interpretation and Overinterpretation* (Cambridge: Cambridge University Press, 1992).

22. Roland Barthes, "Theory of the Text," in Robert Young (ed.), *Untying The Text* (London: Routledge, 1981), pp. 31–47; Julia Kristeva, *Séméiotiké: Recherches pour un sémanalyse* (Paris: Seuil, 1969).

23. Barthes, op. cit., pp. 31–47.

24. Bronislaw Malinowski, *Argonauts of the Western Pacific* (New York: Dutton, 1922); "The Problem of Meaning in Primitive Languages," in C. K. Ogden and I. A. Richards (eds.), *The Meaning of Meaning* (New York: Harcourt, Brace and World, 1923), pp. 2–24.

25. Alfred Radcliffe-Brown, *The Andaman Islanders* (Cambridge: Cambridge University Press, 1922).

26. Joseph L. Henderson, "Ancient Myths and Modern Man," in Carl G. Jung (ed.), *Man and His Symbols* (New York: Dell, 1964), p. 146.

27. Emile Durkheim, *The Elementary Forms of Religious Life* (New York: Collier, 1912).

28. Attilio Bolzoni, *Parole d'onore* (Milano: BUR, 2008), p. 22.

7

Love and Marriage

It is not a lack of love, but a lack of friendship that makes unhappy marriages.
—Friedrich Nietzsche (1844–1900)

Prologue

The song "Love and Marriage Go Together Like a Horse and Carriage," composed by Sammy Cahn and Jimmy van Heusen, and made popular by Frank Sinatra in 1955, encapsulated an unconscious view that love and marriage are inextricable, with the former leading inevitably to the latter. Significantly, the very same song was used in an ironic way as the theme for the TV sitcom *Married with Children*, which ran from 1987 to 1997—a sitcom that tore marriage apart as a failing institution. How did the meaning of marriage change so radically in just a few decades? If love and marriage do indeed go together then why is this so? For the semiotician, to gain any understanding of what something means, it is necessary to unravel how it came into existence in the first place and how it has been represented and conceptualized.

Traditionally, marriage has been tied to other cultural spheres—kinship, religious, economic, etc. The main form of marriage has been endogamy, whereby the members of a community marry within the group. In some societies of the past and even the present, members are formally forbidden from marrying a member of a different clan or group. With the rise of individual choice in matters of the heart, which gained momentum in the chivalric era, the idea that love was the basis for entering into a marriage, not traditions, became an

© The Author(s) 2019
M. Danesi, *The Semiotics of Love*, Semiotics and Popular Culture,
https://doi.org/10.1007/978-3-030-18111-6_7

unconscious principle. In modern times, the same principle of choice has led to the enlargement of the love and marriage equation in an inclusive way—marriage now can take place with partners from different cultural, religious, racial backgrounds, as well as between same-sex partners. Modern marriage is an adaptive social institution, reflecting the changing aspirations and customs of the society in which it is found.[1] But, as argued here, at the core of marriage is love. Indeed, we tend to equate a failed marriage to a "loveless" union, among other factors that may lead to its dissolution.

Marriage and its connection to love is an ideal, a means to make love permanent. The ancient myths, such as the one of Pygmalion (discussed previously), have consistently subscribed to this ideal, recalling that Pygmalion married the woman he had carved out as his ideal, once she came to life. The Romans and other ancient societies also espoused this ideal as a principle in marriage. The Roman tradition of the "kiss of peace" (called the *osculum pacis*) became symbolic of this principle, extending to medieval weddings, which were consummated through the *osculum*—perceived as a spiritual conduit, allowing for the transfer of the souls of the partners into each other. The modern-day nuptial kiss derives from this medieval practice. So, love and marriage have, for a long time, been seen as going together like the proverbial horse and carriage, as the song so poetically puts it. However, representations such as the *Married with Children* sitcom, mirroring various trends in society, have emerged to challenge this idyllic view, reflecting a different perception of marriage. But, despite such critical portrayals, somehow the love-and-marriage equation, like all ideals, is something that we continue to pursue, and the reason may well be that we unconsciously desire to realize the aforementioned principle. There are, of course, other theories of marriage, ranging from its role as a constrainer of otherwise random sexual activities to an institution that provides stability to society, and which will be discussed in this chapter. But the principle adopted here, based on the idealization of love, is a plausible one, given the many stories and images that have ensconced it into communal memory.

Marriage, Love, and Evolution

In most parts of the world, the most common form of marriage is monogamy, the union of two persons, traditionally a man and a woman, so that procreation can be guaranteed (in principle). Indeed, an expression such as "childless couple" brings out the kind of unconscious perception we possess in this domain of culture. Marriage means children, at least traditionally, both to extend the survival of a particular community and to "complete" the love of the partners in the birth of a new life. In some societies, the gender of the partners is no longer relevant, since a legal marriage can be consummated with same-sex partners. But even in such marriages, the desire for a family environment leads the partners typically to seek ways of inserting children into the marriage (through adoption, surrogate childbirth, etc.). No matter what form marriage takes, the point is that love is still expected to be an intrinsic part of the union, a fact that is normally emphasized in the language of the marriage ceremony. The assumption is that idyllic love will give way to family love, embracing children as "springing" from this union—hence the term "offspring." Although this is a guiding emotional principle, there is little doubt that marriage is also a social act, and is thus interconnected with kinship, religion, and other basic institutions that define human cultural life.

In his monumental study of social organization, Charles H. Cooley defined kinship as the primary sphere of a culture, giving sense and perpetuity to the activities of the tribe. As such, marriage functions as a kinship-preserving system.[2] Kinship provides individuals with a primary identity and a vital sense of belonging. This is why people tend to feel a "kinship bond" when they meet a stranger of the same lineal descent, and why, at some point or other in their lives, many individuals tend to become interested in where the "roots" of their "family tree" lead. As the sociologist Max Weber remarked, leadership in early tribal cultures emerged typically from within specific kinship units, because communal activities revolved around the family with the most power and ability to withstand opposition from within the tribe.[3] The central feature of kinship is the primary mother-child bond, to which diverse cultures have added different familial relations by the principle of descent, which connects one generation to the other in a systematic way and which determines certain rights and obligations across generations. Descent groups are traced typically through both partners, that is, bilaterally, or through only the male or the female link, that is, unilaterally. In unilateral systems the descent is known as patrilineal if the derivation is through the male line, or matrilineal if it is through the female line. Anthropological studies of kinship systems have shown that around half of the world's cultures are patrilineal, one-third bilateral, and the remainder matrilineal.[4] Bilateral kinship systems are characteristic of hunting-gathering tribes, such as the !Kung of the Kalahari Desert in southern Africa and the Inuit in northern Canada; but they are now increasingly characteristic of modern societies as well. Other ways for tracing descent are the parallel system, in which males and females each trace their ancestry through their own sex, and the cognatic method, in which the relatives of both sexes are considered, with little formal distinction between them.

The kinship categories are represented by the names (father, aunt, cousin, etc.) given to individuals. These may also indicate how a kinship sphere assigns the inheritance of goods and property. The Iatmul of New Guinea, for instance, assign five different names to the first, second, third, fourth, and fifth child in such a way that in any quarrels over inheritance, the first and third children are expected to join forces against the second and the fourth. A kinship system, in other words, reflects the cultural values and historical experiences of the group; and it is typically connected to the meanings of marriage and family. Whether the marriage is monogamous, polygamous, or polyandrous, it still is embedded in concepts of family and kinship. Today, with second and third marriages becoming almost normal, the emergence of the blended family has come to the forefront, modifying and enlarging the traditional kinship systems. But in all cases, the relation of marriage to family and children is an unconscious principle.

This may well be one of the reasons why marriage is perceived to be a "union" that should withstand adversity, so as to provide stability to the rearing of children—a fact that is symbolized in various ways at weddings. The exchange of rings, called the "wedding bands," is one of these, implying that the spouses should remain united, spiritually and socially. Incidentally, the circular shape of the ring connects it semiotically to the sacred meanings of circles in antiquity, again implying everlasting love (as discussed in the previous chapter). Connected to the sacredness of marriage and family is the color white of the bride's dress—at least in various traditions. As it turns out, this is a fairly recent symbolic practice. Previously, women wore any color or type of dress that they could afford, unless they were part of the nobility or upper classes. It was in 1840, when Queen Victoria married Prince Albert in which she wore a white dress, did white become the symbolic color to wear for weddings. However, that was not the first time that the white wedding dress was worn by an aristocrat. The first documented donning came in 1406, when Philippa of England married Eric of Pomerania. Then in 1559, Mary Queen of Scots wore a white dress at her wedding to Francis, the Dauphin of France, perhaps to symbolize the purity and importance of this event, socially and politically. But the use of white in marriage dresses is not universal. In some traditional regions of China, brides wear a red dress to symbolize joy, as do Indian brides in several areas of India. Now, the origin of the black suit for the groom is not known, despite speculations and urban legends. To a semiotician, this choice reverberates with unconscious oppositional meaning. The white-black, or the clear-versus-dark opposition (*chiaroscuro* in Italian) standing for opposites is an ancient one, and may be the source of the expression "opposites attract." There is no real white or black color on the spectrum of light. Black is absence of color, and when seen together at the same time, the colors on the spectrum appear as white light. However, when light passes through a prism, the different colors separate and can be seen. This suggests that the white-black opposition may have only a conceptual, rather than sensory, origin. So, if the tradition dictates that the bride should wear white, then it is logical semiotically for the groom to wear black.

In effect, all such symbolic artifacts support the principle that love and union are intrinsic to marriage, both for the partners and for the family they are about to have. Of course, things may not turn out as anticipated, but the point is that we *desire* them to turn out ideally. Cultures are based on ideals; without them we would likely be reduced to living by instincts.

Marriage is thus connected with the idea of the infinity of spiritual life, and this is the reason why it has traditionally occurred within a religious sphere, to use Cooley's terminology. The idea that there is life beyond death is a prehistoric one, as borne out by the discovery of the ritualized burial of the dead dating back some 350,000 years. This is a truly extraordinary idea that has dictated the course of human history since ancient times; but why it became an intrinsic feature of human consciousness constitutes a mystifying enigma. Suffice it to say for the present purposes that the notion of a spiritual afterlife is the motivation behind religious beliefs and the related belief that marriage and family are forever, even beyond physical life. Of course, this is, again, an idealistic portrayal, but it is plausible as an explanatory framework for grasping the spiritual meanings that we have assigned to love and marriage. It is not the only one, needless to say. Generally, evolutionary psychologists take a different stance, assigning such beliefs to survival mechanisms. This perspective assumes that the blind forces of evolution have us on a leash, and that human agency does not play any role in shaping our own destiny.

However, a counterargument within psychology and cognitive science, known as *autopoiesis*, has emerged to oppose this perspective. The theory claims that an organism participates in its own evolution, since it has the ability to produce, or at least shape, its various biochemical agents and structures, thus ensuring their efficient and economical operation.[5] In the case of our species, autopoiesis seems to know no bounds. Love is one of its products—it does not emanate exclusively from sexual mechanisms, as the evolutionary theorists might want to claim, since it is often goes against survival, as discussed throughout this book. Evolutionary psychology connects cultural artifacts to survival mechanisms. It sees genetic processes as generative of cultural ones. It is a persuasive form of discourse that fits in with the current tendency to explain consciousness in strictly genetic, rather than historical-cultural-imaginative, terms. Evolutionary psychology basically sees the mind as having the same modular structure of the body, with different adaptations serving different functions. Its main premises are as follows:

- The brain is an information-processing device that translates external inputs into behavioral outputs.
- The brain's adaptive mechanisms are the result of natural and sexual selection.
- The brain has evolved specialized mechanisms to solve recurring problems of survival, which have remained part of the triune brain.
- Most neural processes are unconscious and these enter automatically into the resolution of the problems.

The psychologists have adopted Richard Dawkins' concept of *memes*, defined as units of information that are passed on in cultural environments in order to enhance survivability and promote progress by replacing the functions of genes.[6] Memes are replicating patterns of information (ideas, laws, clothing fashions, artworks, tunes, and so on) and of behavior (marriage rites, courtship rituals, religious ceremonies, and so on) that people inherit directly from their cultural environments. Like genes, memes involve no intentionality on the part of the receiving human organism, which takes them in unreflectively from birth, passing them on just as unreflectively to subsequent generations. The memetic code has thus replaced the genetic code in directing human evolution. In a phrase, memes have emerged in order to help human beings cope with their particular form of life, thus enhancing their collective ability to survive as a species. In this scenario, love is considered to be a convenient meme, serving survival. But as argued throughout this book, and considering the semiotic evidence at hand, from ancient myths and symbols to modern-day rituals, love cannot be easily explained away in memetic-genetic terms—only sex can.

Evolutionary psychology is actually an offshoot of sociobiology. The key figure behind this movement is the North American biologist E. O. Wilson, known for his work tracing the effects of natural selection on biological communities, especially on populations of insects, and for extending the idea of natural selection to human cultures.[7] Since the mid-1950s, Wilson has maintained that social behaviors in humans are genetically based and that evolutionary processes favor those behaviors that enhance reproductive success and survival. Thus, characteristics such as heroism, altruism, aggressiveness, and romantic love should be understood as evolutionary outcomes, not in terms of social or psychic processes. Moreover, Wilson sees the creative capacities undergirding language, art, scientific thinking, myth, etc., as originating in genetic responses that help the human organism survive and continue the species. As he has stated rather bluntly, "no matter how far culture may take us, the genes have culture on a leash."[8]

Like all theoretical paradigms, evolutionary psychology is itself the product of a particular worldview. It is, upon close scrutiny, a contemporary descendant of a philosophical legacy that goes under the rubric of physicalism, which dates back to antiquity. It has simply updated it with a specialized lexicon. Conscious social behaviors are, of course, partially based in biology; but they are not totally so. Genetic factors alone do not completely define human beings. They tell us nothing about why humans create their meaningful experiences and pose the questions they do about life. And they certainly do not explain the enigma of love, equating it with sexual mechanisms which, as argued throughout this book, is not necessarily valid.

The reason why the institutions of marriage and the family are connected to the religious sphere of a culture is hardly based on survival mechanisms. Religion was originally a system of beliefs designed to tie people together, allowing them to express a common sense of purpose beyond immediate life. The term *religion* stems from the Latin word *religio* "to bind, fasten," an etymology that reflects how in early cultures an individual was perceived to be bound by certain mystical or metaphysical (literally "beyond the physical") rites and symbols to the tribe in which the person was reared. To live "unreligiously" would have implied rejecting the tribe's signifying order that bound the members together. The salient feature of early religious belief systems was the absence of any sharp boundary line between the spiritual and the natural worlds, a characteristic that is still found in some modern-day religious practices such as Shinto, a religion practiced in Japan. The Japanese term *Shinto* (from *shin* "spirit") means both "the way of the gods" and "the way of the spirit." The term is also used in common Japanese discourse as an exclamation similar to "Wonderful!" In Shinto, every human being, rock, tree, animal, stream is perceived as having its own wonder. There is no doctrine, creed, or formulated canonical system; Shinto is fundamentally concerned with expressing wonder, respect, and awe for everything that exists. This concern involves treating everything as if it were a person, not in the sense of being inhabited by some human-like ghost or spirit, but in the sense of having a mysterious and independent life of its own that should not be taken for granted.

In an analogical sense, astrology emerged as the counterpart to this animistic belief, aiming to explain the origin of wonders (Chap. 6). The Chaldeans, who lived in Babylon, developed one of the initial forms of astrology as early as 3000 BCE. The Chinese started practicing astrology around 2000 BCE. Other varieties emerged in ancient India and among the Maya of

Central America. Astrology grew out of observations that certain astronomical bodies, particularly the sun and the moon, affected the change of seasons and the success of crops. From such observations, ancient peoples developed a system of metaphysics by which the movements of other bodies such as the planets affected or represented all aspects of life. Love was attributed to astrological forces, leading to perceptions of love as occurring under the influence of the stars or the moon. By around 500 BCE, astrology had spread to Greece, where such philosophers as Pythagoras and Plato incorporated it into their study of religion and the cosmos. Astrology was widely practiced in Europe throughout the Middle Ages, despite its condemnation by the Church. Many scholars of the era viewed astrology and astronomy as complementary sciences until about the 1500s. Only then did the discoveries made by astronomers undermine astrology as a science.

The importance of the religious sphere to the constitution of the love-marriage nexus can be seen in the fact that wizards, priests, and shamans have always tended to be those who officially have consummated a marriage. They have always been thought to have direct contact with supernatural forces, and thus to be endowed with magical powers that allowed them to influence the success of the marriage. In the civilizations of the ancient world, however, religious leaders retained only a part of their authority, having to share power increasingly with secular leaders coming out of the emerging political sphere. With the rise of complex social systems and civilizations these two spheres developed increasingly autonomous, but complementary, functions.

The idea of the love feeling as connected to astrological forces or animistic principles has certainly been a factor in making marriage a spiritual institution, rather than just a socially-convenient one. When individuals started to experiment with love feelings independently of tribal practices, as the early myths indicated, a broader and more personal view of spirituality emerged. As a consequence, people in love tended to develop a marked sense of demarcation between their feelings and the natural world—a feeling that through love they could conquer anything in that world. This perception continues to be a part even of modern-day secular societies, where love is seen as empowering and emboldening people to confront anything in life. It would not be a stretch to claim that our modern-day concepts of identity and individual choice derive, ultimately, from the sense that love is a liberating force. This is a constant subtext in all semiotic products of love, from the ancient myths to the current symbolic practices, as discussed throughout this book. This is, in fact, an implicit code sustaining and informing literature, art, and social institutions. Anyone who has not had access to this love code, will simply not understand our love stories. The signifying order is built from this code, diffusing its meanings throughout the entire social system. Because it reverberates with archetypal senses, it is likely to be a universal or "master code," as evidenced by similar, analogous, or isomorphic representational and symbolic practices connected to love and marriage throughout the world.

The master code may also be the force behind the emergence of philosophy and the arts, separating love and marriage from the strictly religious and kinship spheres, as can already be seen in Plato, who attempted to reconcile the spheres by proposing a model of a community that would be governed by "philosopher-kings," capable of decoding inherent principles of human life.[9] It was Aristotle who recognized the ever-increasing power of the political, legal, and economic spheres in city-state cultures. In his *Politics*, he suggested that these were often in conflict with the religious sphere because of the tension created by their overlapping moral jurisdictions.[10] Gradually, marriage became part of the political-legal sphere overlapping with the religious one. At the same time that the philosophers and rulers were discussing marriage as a necessary social institution, the storytellers were subtly portraying it as a master code for understanding ourselves and even the cosmos.

Marriage in Contemporary Perspective

The foregoing discussion was meant to emphasize that love and marriage have always been expected to go together, in an ideal world, even if the reality is a different one; and this has nothing to do with survival of the species. In many of the myths, poetry, legends, narratives, etc. based on true love, marriage is not even a necessary outcome of love, including in fairytales, since the final kiss is not typically followed up by marriage. Most of the legendary crimes of passion actually arise from betrayals and love trysts between married or betrothed persons. This does not mean that love and marriage are mutually exclusive; on the contrary, they often congeal into a unity of heart and soul, to use a common cliché. In the contemporary world, we still expect them to go together, and when they do not, then divorce, separation, or some other form of severance is expected.

One way to assess how the perception of the love and marriage equation is unfolding in the contemporary world is to examine some of the modern-day sitcoms that deal with it. If there is one sitcom that espoused a cynical view of marriage as an idyllic mode of love, it was *Seinfeld* in the 1990s. The program reflected the gradually declining importance of marriage in society, questioning the goal of raising a family, and of seeking to make something of oneself in life in accordance with the American Dream. Is there really anything worth striving for other than daily survival? The characters in the sitcom did not subscribe to the narrative of marriage, family, and career as indexes of success. They lived day-to-day with no goals other than exchanging repartees among themselves. The sitcom painted a picture of marriage as irrelevant and even counterproductive to romance. The sitcom was a self-styled "show about nothing." It ran from 1989 to 1998, an era characterized as postmodern, a view of life as a series of meaningless events and episodes that really never coalesce into defining any purpose to existence. The characters rejected the model of love-and-marriage-go-together-like-a-horse-and-carriage with effective comedy, capturing the attention of large audiences of the same age demographic as the actors. Similar portraits of marriage were painted by sitcoms such as *Married with Children* (as mentioned), *Three and a Half Men*, *Friends*, *The Simpsons*, and others. These stood in contrast to the "happy family" sitcoms of the 1950s, such as *Father Knows Best* and *Ozzie and Harriet*. *The Simpsons* started in 1987 as a weekly feature on the Tracey Ullman television show, debuting as a separate program in 1989. It was a satire of bourgeois American life and especially of the middle-class family and its self-serving values. It also critiqued many aspects of contemporary society and its pretentions. Its portrayal of the "typical" family was sardonic at best, and highly ludicrous at worst. The family stayed together, not because of love, but because this was the way people lived, whether they liked it or not.

The sitcom genre started in the early radio era; it was an adaptation of the Commedia dell'Arte (Chap. 2), which dealt with love trysts, romance, marriage and family relations in humorous, satirical ways. Since the outset, the sitcoms explored the same kind of themes in a similarly comedic and farcical manner. In early 1950s television, Lucille Ball's *I Love Lucy* dealt with the battle of the sexes, neighbor conflicts, and especially the relevance of marriage to society as a stabilizing force, no matter the imperfections of the partners, as did the Commedia dell'Arte. *The Honeymooners* showed the reality of a lower middle class family and the challenges that marriage presented to the characters—there was no sugar-coating there, just the harsh reality of daily arguments and constant disagreements; but in the end the couple remained faithful showing an abiding love for each other—a constant theme in the Commedia dell'Arte as well.

A sitcom that dealt with love and marriage in a new imaginative way was the *Big Bang Theory*, which premiered in 2007. The two main characters, Leonard and Sheldon, are physicists. Penny became their neighbor. She was a waitress and aspiring actress. The engineer Howard and astrophysicist Raj were geeky coworkers of Leonard and Sheldon. Other characters were scripted into the sitcom in subsequent years, including romantic partners for Sheldon and Howard. In the end, marriages were consummated between the characters—Leonard and Penny, Sheldon and Amy, Howard and Bernadette. Dating and romance emerged spontaneously among these characters, suggesting that love and marriage are alive and well, no matter who the partners are. Clearly, the love-and-marriage equation is undergoing modification, but it is still a reality arguably because it is based on the unconscious master code that has always directed human destiny.

As our stories and even comedies suggest, love has nothing to do with survival instincts. Even in ludicrous situations, it is obvious that once we catch the love bug, we become ourselves deconstructive, willing to leave everything behind. Love simply does not fit in with any of the theories of species survival. Movies like *The Notebook* (2004) revolve around the idea that marriage is a means of making love permanent and stable. Despite its sentimentality, it captures the same subtext of the Paolo and Francesca tale—love cannot be denied or suppressed by time or anything else.

Prelude to Marriage

Not too long ago, if a "boy met a girl" and they started dating regularly, the relation would have soon turned into something more serious. The terms "fiancé" and "fiancée" would then have been used to indicate that the romantic deal was about to be sealed, symbolized of course with an engagement ring. This type of relation meant several common things to each romantic partner—fidelity to each other, planning for marriage and children, and mapping out a future together. Things could go wrong along the way, of course, but the cultural environment in which the two romantic partners lived encouraged the expectation that marriage was the vehicle for guaranteeing a "happily ever after" relationship.

Today this paradigm is seen much more skeptically, as *Seinfeld* clearly showed, whereby marriage, family and long-term plans together are not necessarily aspirations in what can be called the "prelude to marriage," rather than dating or courtship, which reverberate with historical meanings that may no longer hold, at least in the same way. The rules of romance and commitment have changed. Matchmaking now occurs both in the real world and the hyperreal world of the Internet, leading to a new kind of obsession over love and marriage, different (yet somewhat similar) to the obsession of which the ancient Greeks spoke and which became part of early legends. There are now myriads of self-help manuals, websites, television and radio programs, giving advice on how to "find the right mate," indicating that people are still looking for the magical solution to solving the mystery of love. In the past, stories of "elixirs of love" were common for the same reason.

As Cristina Nehring has documented, we may have lost our sense of idyllic romance under the stars in this new age of love apps and expedient relations, but that does not mean that romance is dead.[11] Her study showed that aspirations of love are still strong motivators in any prelude to marriage. Similarly, Donna Freitas found that many people actually revile hook-up culture, even if they become embroiled in it, because of the lack of love within such relations.[12] In a phrase, sex without love is unfulfilling, as the ancients certainly knew. In hook-ups, the love relationship is expected to be short-lived, sexually-based, and then discarded as easily as it was contracted. But this leads to disappointment and lack of fulfillment, as the studies now indicate. Perhaps the casual nature of hook-ups is unconsciously aimed at avoiding "broken hearts" or tearful breakups—that is, if things do not work out, then we can easily depart from the relationship with few emotional repercussions. A study by DeLecce and Weisfeld looked at the factors that lead to breakups in nonmarital relations, providing an interesting angle from which to view this type of prelude behavior.[13] The researchers found that women were significantly more likely to report feeling happy after a breakup, while men were more likely to report feeling sexually frustrated following dissolution. What is remarkable about the study is the role reversal in love relations when compared to previous gendered models.

In sum, it seems that love and romance cannot congeal from hook-ups, but that we still seek it despite the available opportunities for sex alone. Romance requires involvement and creative commitment. The problem may well be that our idyllic love stories envision love as unfolding in a "perfect" world, while dating and marriage occur in an "imperfect one." If we are not aware of this—that is, of the distinction between fantasy and reality (Chap. 4)—then failure in relationships is virtually inevitable. Thousands of stories are still being told that are based on the blueprint of the Paolo and Francesca or Romeo and Juliet tales, in which true love shatters the habitual, makes us forget mundane arguments, jealousies, and all the other hassles that make up everyday life. Whether this is realistic or not, it is in our emotional makeup.

As mentioned, the obsession with relationships today is obvious on the many "dating and advice" blogs and websites that deal with romance. Some titles are truly interesting in this regard, indicating in compressed form what our concerns and emphases are today. The following are all taken from websites (many of which have already dissipated into the ether of cyberspace): "Porn Watching Changes the Male Brain," "Reasons to Avoid Marriage," "Marrying Down Encouraged for Women," "Importance of Romance," "Gender Equality in Marriage Means Less Sex," "Divorce Is Not an Option," "Impact of Technology on Relationships," among myriad others. Matchmaking and hook-ups have also migrated to cyberspace on sites such as OkCupid, PlentyOfFish, and

Match or apps like Tinder, Grindr, and Scruff. But there is nothing new here. In the past, a hook-up would have been called a "one night stand" and match-making involved random meetings at locales such as dance halls and pubs. So, the contemporary notion of love as something to be negotiated through some conduit or location is really nothing more than an update on previous types of encounters. Hook-up culture has been a popular media story for the last few years. But, it is merely an updated version of previous narratives.

In fact, stories from the past about affairs and trysts were actually hook-ups that led to unwanted consequences. Take the story of Guinevere and Sir Lancelot du Lac, discussed previously. Guinevere was the wife of the legendary King Arthur of Britain. She appears first in the twelfth-century *Historia* cycle of Arthurian romances by English chronicler Geoffrey of Monmouth. It was, however, the French poet Chrétien de Troyes who introduced the story of the tragic love affair between Guinevere and Lancelot to the world. After marrying Arthur, Guinevere is smitten by Lancelot, a handsome knight of the court in Camelot. It is their adulterous relationship that eventually brings about the unraveling of Camelot and the downfall of Arthur. The painting below, which was created in the nineteenth century, depicts the hidden and foreboding power of illicit love, taking place in a forest—a metaphor for fear and darkness (Fig. 7.1):

"And then they rode to the divided way, there kiss'd, and parted weeping."

Fig. 7.1 *Lancelot and Guinevere's Parting Kiss (George Wooliscroft and Louis Rhead, 1898)* (Wikimedia Commons)

The first encounter between the two star-crossed lovers is actually orchestrated by Lancelot's friend Galahad, and is recorded by the *Arthurian Romances* as follows: "And the queen sees that the knight dares not do more, so she takes him by the chin and kisses him in front of Galahad for quite a long time."[14] It was, to use contemporary phraseology, a hook-up arranged through a friend. As the French expression goes, *plus ça change, plus c'est la même chose* (the more it changes, the more it is the same).

Every culture deals with the prelude period in specific ways. The common theme in all of them is that sex without love is ultimately unfulfilling. Prelude romantic behavior may have migrated to the online world, but its goals have remained the same. The premise in online dating is that algorithms are better predictors of successful romance and eventually marriage success than are human matchmakers or the random efforts of people falling in love. The traditional notion of love as occurring "at first sight" and thus unpredictable has been replaced with love occurring "post hoc," that is after the match has been made by the algorithm. But the irony is that online matchmaking has hardly solved the problem of love and its role in successful marriage; algorithms have not solved the mystery of romance.

Robot Lovers

It is mindboggling to think that there is today a substantive demand for robot lovers, which is growing with new businesses that are working to give people the robot lovers they want. Of course, this could well be nothing more than a modern form of fetishism, since people have fallen in love with dolls and other objects in the past. As we have seen, iconicity—resemblance in form and function—is a persuasive force in human cognition. Lifelike robots are iconic forms that allow for fantasy love to be imagined and performed, recalling, again, the Pygmalion myth. In 2016, computer scientists in China created a lifelike robot that acts, behaves, talks, and responds sexually like a human female companion. They called her Jia Jia; she follows orders, and has human-like facial expressions. The theme of robot or artificial love is now a common one in movies, such as *Her* (2014), in which a man, heartbroken by a failed marriage, falls in love with an operating system, which appears to return his love. But there is no love algorithm that can ever be devised—in *Her* it is the male's aspirations that are at work, interpreting the computer's input in romantic terms; and in robots such as Jia Jia it is the human lover himself who, like Pygmalion, enacts love in his imagination through iconicity. It also implies an inner need to control the outcome of love. This theme was treated brilliantly by Bryan Forbes in his 1975 movie, *The Stepford Wives*. The female characters find themselves trapped in a patriarchal world and decide to rebel against it. The men of Stepford, fed up with their requests, replace them with lifelike robots that are programmed to do anything they ask of them. When one of the men is asked why they would do such a monstrous thing, his reply is: "Because we can." The movie is a black comedy, playing on male fears as well as on the modern-day skepticism related to marriage.

The need to reproduce life in material form is ancient. In Sumerian and Babylonian myths there were accounts of the creation of life through the animation of clay. The ancient Romans were also fascinated by the creation of automata that could replace many human activities. By the time of Mary Shelley's *Frankenstein* in 1818, the idea that robots could be brought to life and seek love on their own both fascinated and horrified the imagination. Since the turn of the twenty-first century the quest to animate nonbiological machines has been relentless. It has captured the imagination of a large segment of our image-makers. Movie robots and humanoid machines have all the attributes of gods. As William Barrett remarks, if a machine will ever be built with the features of the human mind it would have "a curiously disembodied kind of consciousness, for it would be without the sensitivity, intuitions, and pathos of our human flesh and blood. And without those qualities we are less than wise, certainly less than human."[15] One cannot underestimate the power of the human imagination to literally create mind worlds. Robot love is an imaginative construct—a need to tame love and make it manageable. It provides a literal interpretation to the love-machine metaphor discussed previously.

The last assertion is one of the thematic subtexts of the 1982 movie *Blade Runner*, directed by Ridley Scott, based on a science fiction story titled *Do Androids Dream of Electric Sheep?* by Philip K. Dick in which a dehumanized society is dominated by technology and science. What if we could bring machines to life and thus allow them to experience love in the human sense? What would they be like? Would they be more "human" than humans? Against the depressing backdrop of a contemporary choking urban landscape, Rick Deckard is one of a select few futuristic law-enforcement officers, nicknamed "blade runners," who have been trained to detect and track down "replicants," powerful humanoid robots who have been engineered to do the work of people in space. But the replicants have gone amok. They have somehow developed self-awareness and have started to seek immortality. A desperate band of these killer replicants has made its way back to earth aiming to have their programs changed, looking desperately for the sinister corporate tycoon responsible for their creation so that he can reprogram them to extend their life eternally. Deckard's assignment is to track down these runaway robots and terminate them.

His search takes place in an urban wasteland where punk mutants control the streets while the pathetic inhabitants of endless blocks of gloomy high-rises remain glued to their TV sets. Deckard relies on a video cassette recorder (VCR), complete with stop action and precision image-enhancers, to find the replicants through dark alleys abandoned to the forces of anarchy. He identifies a captured suspect as being either "human" or "replicant" with the classic Turing Test used by artificial intelligence theorists. Shortly before his untimely death in his early 1950s, Turing suggested that one could program a computer in such a way that it would be virtually impossible to discriminate between its answers and those contrived by a human being. His notion has become immortalized as the Turing Test. It goes somewhat like this. Suppose a human observer is placed in a room that hides a computer on one side and, on the other, another human being. The computer and human being can only respond to questions in writing on pieces of paper which are passed back and forth from the observer to the computer and human being through slits in the wall. If the observer cannot identify, on the basis of the written responses, who is the computer and who the human being, then the observer must conclude that the machine is "intelligent." It has passed the Turing Test. Deckard's detection technique is similar, but it transcends the test, because he focuses on the reactions of his interviewee's eyes to his questions, which convey emotion. Replicants use their artificial eyes exclusively to see; humans use them both to see and to show feeling. Aware of the mysterious power of the human eye, the replicants kill their maker by poking out his eyes. Interestingly, we are never sure throughout the movie if Deckard is a human or a replicant himself, since the camera never provides a close-up of his eyes.

In this postmodern scenario, Deckard falls in love with one of the replicants, Rachel, whose name has obvious intertextual connections with the Biblical character of the same name. She helps him track down his prey, falling in love with him as well. The film makes many other references to the Bible and Christian love. Near the end, a naked replicant, Roy, with only a white cloth around his waist, in obvious allusion to the Crucifixion scene, saves Deckard's life at the cost of his own. The white dove that appears when Roy "expires" is reminiscent of the dove that was sent to Noah's ark in the midst of torrential rain to help the ark find a safe place away from the deluge—a symbolic quest for a safer future. That is, in fact, what happens right after Roy's demise, as Deckard and Rachel escape the gruesome city scene to fly off into the countryside. The dark, gloomy atmosphere suddenly clears up, the sun comes out, and a "new dawn" rises. These are images that call to mind the Garden of Eden scene.

Blade Runner asks the fundamental questions of philosophy in a new way: What is a human being? What is love and why is it a distinguishing feature of humanity? A sequel directed by Denis Villeneuve was released in 2017, titled *Blade Runner 2049*, in which a blade runner, named K, discovers a secret that has the potential of plunging humankind into total chaos. This leads him on a quest to find the original blade runner, Rick Deckard, who has been missing for thirty years. The movie is interesting on two counts. First, it resurrects the future, so to speak, by bringing it to the present. More importantly the date in the title, 2049, is highly suggestive of computer engineer Ray Kurzweil's prediction that a technological "singularity" will occur around that year, when the replicants will have surpassed natural human intelligence.[16]

In the end, love among the robots is a sci-fi construct. Love cannot be "algorithmicized;" not can it be "biologized," since it is not a biological or neural system that can be identified as separate from other systems. This view is in line with the work of biologist-semiotician Jakob von Uexküll.[17] Von Uexküll suggested that the world of objects and information (the *Umwelt*) is perceived in a particular way by a species via the particular neural-anatomical structures with which it is endowed by nature, and that this allows the species to construct its own models of that world (the *Innenwelt*) so as to be able to understand it on its own terms and thus cope with it. In the case of humans, the modeling process is a sophisticated one that involves abstract symbolism. This is why humans do not simply react to stimuli; they interact inventively, creatively, and symbolically with them. They change stimuli into sign forms of the world that then can be used to further explore that world. This means, ultimately, that humans are in charge of their own evolution, as the autopoietic movement in cognitive science now suggests (as discussed previously).[18] Love is autopoietic, allowing humans to shape their own life schemes, in partnership with nature. As Marshall McLuhan once remarked, we live in "a man-made environment that transfers the evolutionary process from biology to technology."[19] This is why robot lovers seem so credible to us—we *made* them.

Epilogue

Will romantic love survive in an age where we can get anything we want with a click of a computer mouse, a voice command, or a quick touch of the screen? As argued throughout this book, the answer is a resounding yes. One could even claim ostensibly that we have entered a second era of courtly love. In the medieval era, a man in love with a woman of equally high, or higher, birth had to prove his devotion by heroic deeds and amorous writings. Once the lovers had exchanged pledges and consummated their passion, complete secrecy had to be maintained. Since most noble marriages of the time were little more than business contracts, courtly love was a form of sanctioned escapism. The patterns of courtly lovemaking spread throughout society, turning romance into an art form. The sign of this was that poets and musicians became obsessed with the theme of love. The same obsession can be seen throughout social media sites. Romance, betrayal, sex and the other themes that made the troubadour songs of the era popular are still around. The language has been updated, but the semantics is the same. As the twentieth century American social critic Emma Goldman wrote: "Rather would I have the love songs of romantic ages, rather Don Juan and Madame Venus, rather an elopement by ladder and rope on a moonlight night, followed by the father's curse, mother's moans, and the moral comments of neighbors, than correctness and propriety measured by yardsticks."[20]

Marriage will last since it is more than just an economic arrangement; it is still perceived as a promise that love can last forever. As novelist Dan Brown has so aptly put it, love cannot be invented or controlled; it is something beyond human governance[21]:

Love is from another realm. We cannot manufacture it on demand. Nor can we subdue it when it appears. Love is not our choice to make.

Computer programs designed to simulate human intelligence are becoming more and more sophisticated, and will likely lead to the singularity of mind; but not of love. Computer programs designed to simulate romantic love can be written of course; but when a computer is asked what love is, it can only answer according to its algorithm. Human love is non-algorithmic; it is something whose meaning is elusive.

Coming to the end of our semiotic story of love and a search for its origins and meaning through semiotic artifacts, from language to painting and technology, the only conclusion that is achievable is a disappointing one—love remains a mystery, and no one theory can ever pin down its source. It emanates from the body; it is a paradox connected to sexual and survival urges; it is part of how we perceive ourselves as more than physical organic substance; and on and on. But it is more than all of these combined. It is not a simple cultural construction, since it is found universally as a force across cultures, suggesting that it transcends them. Its universality is why the different representations that have been devised for it, from myths to paintings, strike a resoundingly similar emotional chord in people, no matter what language they speak or what culture they have been raised in. It also bears a deep message within it—love is an antidote to hate, and all the nefarious events that hatred has produced throughout history. There is no other way to conquer vengeance effectively. And yet, why this is so remains a deep mystery. The following lines from Kahlil Gibran's marvelous poetic treatment of love, *The Prophet*, constitute a fitting ending to our semiotic foray[22]:

Love gives naught but itself and takes naught but from itself.
Love possesses not nor would it be possessed;
For love is sufficient unto love.
When you love you should not say, "God is in my heart," but rather, "I am in the heart of God."
And think not you can direct the course of love, if it finds you worthy, directs your course.
Love has no other desire but to fulfill itself.

Notes

1. A good overview of marriage and love customs is the one by Carolyn Mordecai, *Weddings: Dating & Love Customs of Cultures Worldwide, Including Royalty* (Phoenix: Nittany, 1999).
2. Charles H. Cooley, *Social Organization* (New York: Scribner, 1909).
3. Max Weber, *Economy and Society* (New York: Simon and Schuster, 1922).
4. See Ladislav Holy, *Anthropological Perspectives of Kinship* (London: Pluto Press, 1996).
5. Humberto R. Maturana and Francisco Varela, *Autopoiesis and Cognition: The Realization of the Living* (Dordrecht: Reidel, 1973).
6. See Richard Dawkins, *The Selfish Gene* (Oxford: Oxford University Press, 1976); *Unweaving the Rainbow: Science, Delusion and the Appetite for Wonder* (Boston: Houghton Mifflin, 1998).
7. E. O. Wilson, *Sociobiology: The New Synthesis* (Cambridge, Mass.: Harvard University Press, 1975); *On Human Nature* (New York: Bantam, 1979); *Biophilia* (Cambridge, Mass.: Harvard University Press, 1984); E. O. Wilson and M. Harris, "Heredity versus Culture: A Debate," in J. Guillemin (ed.), *Anthropological Realities: Reading in the Science of Culture*, pp. 450–465 (New Brunswick, NJ: Transaction Books, 1984).
8. Wilson and Harris, op. cit., p. 464.
9. Plato, *The Republic* (Open Road Media, 2014, orig. 281 BCE).
10. Aristotle, *Politics* (Nuvision Publications, 2004, orig. 4th century BCE).

11. Cristina Nehring, *A Vindication of Love: Reclaiming Romance for the Twenty-First Century* (New York: HarperCollins, 2009).

12. Donna Freitas, *The End of Sex* (New York: Basic Books, 2013).

13. Tara DeLecce and Glenn Weisfeld, "An Evolutionary Explanation for Sex Differences in Nonmarital Breakup Experiences," *Adaptive Human Behavior and Physiology* (2015): https://doi.org/10.1007/s40750-015-0039-z.

14. Chrétien de Troyes, *Arthurian Romances* (Courier Corporation, 2006), p. 34.

15. William Barrett, *The Death of the Soul: From Descartes to the Computer* (New York: Anchor, 1986), p. 160.

16. Ray Kurzweil, *The Singularity Is Near* (Harmondsworth: Penguin, 2005); *How to Create a Mind: The Secret of Human Thought Revealed* (New York: Viking, 2012).

17. Jakob von Uexküll, *Umwelt und Innenwelt der Tierre* (Berlin: Springer, 1909).

18. Humberto R. Maturana and Francisco Varela, *Autopoiesis and Cognition: The Realization of the Living* (Dordrecht: Reidel, 1973).

19. Marshall McLuhan, *Through the Vanishing Point* (New York: Harper & Row, 1968), p. 85.

20. Emma Goldman, *Anarchism and Other Essays* (London: Fifield, 1910), p. 23.

21. Dan Brown, *Origin* (New York: Anchor, 2017), pp. 590–591.

22. Kahlil Gibran, *The Prophet* (New York: Alfred A. Knopf, 1923).

Index

© The Author(s) 2019
M. Danesi, *The Semiotics of Love*, Semiotics and Popular Culture,
https://doi.org/10.1007/978-3-030-18111-6